Will You
Give Me a
Reading?

About the Author

Jenna Matlin, MS, is a full-time tarot practitioner who marries the science of psychology with the art of intuition to create deeply moving oracular experiences. Since her tarot business launched in 2012, she was awarded Best of Philly: "Spiritual Guru" by *Philadelphia Magazine* in 2019 and has been featured in various online spaces such as Buzzfeed and Bustle.

Jenna has authored two previous books, *Have Tarot Will Party* and *Have Tarot Will Travel*, and she presents at tarot conferences both domestically and abroad. Jenna enjoys working with clients such as Urban Outfitters and Crate and Barrel, in addition to reading for and teaching to tarot enthusiasts around the world.

Jenna is known for being a creative force in the tarot community with her distinctive style of reading and dedication to the art of delivering truly helpful sessions. Jenna's other interests include all things nature and writing poetry on wild full moon nights. "Hedge Witch" would certainly describe Jenna, and her cats agree. To find out more, visit www.jennamatlin.com.

Praise for Will You Give Me a Reading?

"An excellent resource for new readers and seasoned ones alike. Jenna breaks down all the most common questions and situations a reader may encounter and offers sage advice…There are many well-thought-out and easy-to-do energy exercises to incorporate into your everyday workings. This is a brilliant book to add to your tarot toolbox and will help any reader build a sound foundation for a great tarot practice."

—Jen Sankey, author of *Stardust Wanderer Tarot*

"There are many books on the market that teach you the basics of tarot reading, but not too many that show you how to string the cards together to form a cohesive and helpful narrative. Jenna Matlin has bridged that much-needed gape…This is a master course on the art of tarot reading and guaranteed to help both new readers and pros. Jenna leaves no card unturned. Everything you might encounter is covered, including predictions, empathy, court cards, and challenging situations."

—Theresa Reed, author of *Tarot: No Questions Asked*

"Jenna Matlin's gem of a book is the cool yet reassuring guidance of the tarot sister you always wish you had. Jenna guides you along the star-sprinkled path of tarot and you'll be reading confidently in no time!"

—Sasha Graham, author of *The Magic of Tarot*

"Where was this book when I was fist starting out? This is the question I kept asking all the way through this practical step by step pager turner of a book! A must-have for all who want to start their reader journey."

—Leeza Robertson, creator of the *Mermaid Tarot*

"Written in Jenna's down to earth yet erudite style and chock-full of exercises, anecdotes, and tips that stem from her more than 30 years of experience, this book is the perfect tool for exploring the different dynamics that play a significant role in reading tarote…Matlin allows the reader to put theory to test and make their own discoveries along the way while providing continued guidance and support throughout the text."

—Chris Onaero, tarot professional and host of *We're Booked*

"THIS is the book I wish I had when I first began reading tarot professionally! If I'd had this gem of a book in my hot little hands when I started out as a reader, I would have saved myself a lot of mistakes and wouldn't have had to learn the hard way!"

—Kate Fisher, founder of Daily Tarot Girl

"This book is chock-full of really good ideas—from the practical to the spiritual, based on her extraordinarily thoughtful wisdom and care for both the client and the reader. You can't go wrong with this brilliant book."

—James Divine, palmist, mystic, and joy monger

"Matlin's background in organizational psychology brings a whole new set of tools to the table. She offers clear, detailed advice on how to read the cards as a cohesive whole. Learn how to interpret your layout as a narrative rather than one card by one card. Your clients will get deeper responses to their questions and you will feel like a rock stare…*Will You Give Me A Reading* is your map to taking your tarot from basic to brilliant."

—Arwen Lynch-Poe, author, teacher, psychic, and medium

"A treasure trove of fantastic tips to take your readings to the next level. Good for any level, this book will leave you feeling confident to begin reading for others, or to push yourself to go deeper with your client's questions."

—Jaymi Elford, author of *Tarot Inspired Life*

"A brilliant roadmap in developing one's own language of tarot and in trusting oneself as a reader. Under the impressive skill and deep care of Matlin's hard-earned experience, this entire book winds through the complex interplay of the energies of reading with flow and claritye…Matlin's love and devotion of tarot is extraordinary. Her generosity in sharing this is worth its weight in gold."

—Nancy C. Antenucci, author of *Tarot Rituals*

What You Need to Read Tarot with Confidence

Will You Give Me a Reading?

Foreword by Benebell Wen

JENNA MATLIN

Llewellyn Publications
Woodbury, Minnesota

FIRST EDITION
Second Printing, 2023

Book design by Christine Ha
Cover design by Kevin R. Brown
Cover illustration by Yulia Vysotskaya
Editing by Laura Kurtz
Interior art by the Llewellyn Art Department
Tarot card illustrations are from the *Tarot Original 1909 Deck* by Pamela Colman Smith and
    Arthur Edward Waite. Used with permission of LoScarabeo s.r.l.

Llewellyn Publications is a registered trademark of Llewellyn Worldwide Ltd.

Library of Congress Cataloging-in-Publication Data

Names: Matlin, Jenna, author.
Title: Will you give me a reading? : what you need to read tarot with
    confidence / Jenna Matlin.
Description: Woodbury, Minnesota : Llewellyn Publications, 2022. | Includes
    bibliographical references. | Summary: "For people who already or would
    like to begin reading tarot for others, advice on how to handle yourself
    and the querent, including common issues that come up. Includes
    anecdotes, example readings, and spreads"-- Provided by publisher.
Identifiers: LCCN 2022036873 (print) | LCCN 2022036874 (ebook) | ISBN
    9780738770109 (paperback) | ISBN 9780738770413 (ebook)
Subjects: LCSH: Tarot. | Tarot cards.
Classification: LCC BF1879.T2 M375 2022 (print) | LCC BF1879.T2 (ebook) |
    DDC 133.3/2424--dc23/eng/20220908
LC record available at https://lccn.loc.gov/2022036873
LC ebook record available at https://lccn.loc.gov/2022036874

Llewellyn Worldwide Ltd. does not participate in, endorse, or have any authority or responsibility concerning private business transactions between our authors and the public.

All mail addressed to the author is forwarded but the publisher cannot, unless specifically instructed by the author, give out an address or phone number.

Any internet references contained in this work are current at publication time, but the publisher cannot guarantee that a specific location will continue to be maintained. Please refer to the publisher's website for links to authors' websites and other sources.

Llewellyn Publications
A Division of Llewellyn Worldwide Ltd.
2143 Wooddale Drive
Woodbury, MN 55125-2989
www.llewellyn.com

Printed in the United States of America

Author's Note

The stories in this book are illustrative highlights from real clients and tarot readers. However, their words and stories have been altered. Some stories are composites of several different situations to highlight particular points, while others have had descriptive characteristics rewritten to preserve anonymity.

Contents

Foreword

Few can balance the mystical and the practical as well as Jenna Matlin does. With a master of science degree in organizational psychology, she navigates the empirical world with ease and in principle has always been a rational skeptic. Yet she is psychic and clairvoyant, possessing an extra-sensory knowledge of the unseen world. She keenly understands that there is more to our reality than what we can observe or prove.

It is rare to find an author of a tarot book who harmonizes logic and intuition, and that's what *Will You Give Me a Reading?* presents to you: a step-by-step guide to master delivery of a card reading with examples from real life experiences on how to excel as a professional tarot reader. For decades, Matlin has successfully operated an in-person tarot business. She had an online presence before online tarot became a trend, and she is considered one of the early pioneers in teaching business skills and marketing to tarot professionals. Now Matlin distills her wellspring of knowledge and experience into a handbook of advice that will jumpstart your learning curve.

The book begins by addressing an issue I struggled with: deciding when the right moment would be to let people in your life, especially work colleagues or deeply religious friends, know that you are a tarot reader. Here's another insecurity many can relate to: How do you know if you're psychic? How does one go about honing their psychic abilities anyway? Psychic ability might be likened to instinct, and the psychic-mystic is a universal archetype that you can self-actualize. Matlin describes psychic ability as "an evolutionary adaptation for survival."

When you start reading the cards for others, inevitably a rapid series of synchronicities begin to happen, and you'll find querents repeatedly asking you, "How did you know that?" It begs the question: How much of our lives is fated, and how much of it is left up to free will? What is the role of pre-determinism, determinism, and indeterminism? These difficult philosophical inquiries are covered in her book as theoretical principles the learned tarot reader will want to explore.

There are so few intermediate tarot books. Beginner books that go through card meanings are a dime a dozen, but a well-written intermediate text that deep-dives into the bones and spirit of a card reading is hard to find. *Will You Give Me a Reading?* has filled that gap. From understanding how to interpret those ever-tricky court cards as a person, an action, or a psychological state, to a chronological step-by-step guide to how a reading is conducted, and how to read with both compassion and integrity, you'll want to reread this book every few years just to keep your reading skills sharpened.

Matlin's book comes to us in prescient times, just as the number of online professional tarot startups has gone on the rise. The year of the global quarantine was a prodigious year in growth for tarot home businesses, life coaching, and spiritual consulting. A resurging mainstream interest in tarot, astrology, shamanism, and chakras has also grown. The market potential of reading tarot for others is flourishing at a rapid rate.

Mastering the ability to read tarot for others has become a much sought-after skill, and yet well-vetted texts that will help navigate such entrepreneurial waters are scarce, which is why Matlin is a treasure. *Will You Give Me a Reading?* is a great prerequisite for anyone looking to become a tarot professional. Her signature two-part twelve-step layering tarot technique is brilliant. Mastering that technique is what will set you apart as a reader.

While writing my inaugural text, *Holistic Tarot*, back in 2012, I reached out to Matlin for discussions on tarot subjects, and we immediately became friends. Over the years we've confided in each other, consulted each other on professional matters, and shared stories over good food and wine at tarot conferences. I've known her for almost a decade, and in all that time, she has shown herself to be loyal, kind, considerate, and exactly the type of tarot reader anyone would want in their corner. Matlin commands an impressive depth and breadth of tarot knowledge, which you'll never see her boasting about, because she is grounded, down-to-earth, and unpretentious. I can think of no one better qualified to write this book.

Once you have learned the card meanings and attained fluency over the tarot language, how do you operate the system in a way that will guide others in matters of the heart, in evaluating career options, and help to navigate them toward realizing their life purpose? In *Will You Give Me a Reading?* Jenna Matlin is the voice of a wise mentor who will refine your tarot skills, show you how to structure a tarot reading session, and master control over the flow of your readings. To the tarot reader seeking to gain confidence in how you read the cards, may this book be your pathfinder.

Benebell Wen
Author of *Holistic Tarot* and
creator of the *Spirit Keeper's Tarot*

Introduction

There is nothing like giving someone a reading so helpful that it changes their very own relationship to life. Like teachers, tarot readers find meaning when we see our querents have "aha" moments. We delight in seeing our readings provide relief and find joy when we are able to help someone with a crossroads moment. But being able to do this well takes more than just reading the cards. Good readers for others have a whole grimoire of techniques at their disposal, and reading tarot is only one part. The good news is this: these skills can be learned at any tarot level.

There are also moments where our readings do not help in the ways we hope or we feel our querents are not hearing what the reading is saying. Learning why this happens and what to do about it builds confidence and resilience for you as a reader. Hint: most of the time it has nothing to do with you or your reading!

So if you are asking yourself whether your tarot level is right for *Will You Give Me a Reading?*, the answer is yes! You are welcome here if you are totally new to tarot, if you are returning to tarot after a long break, or if traditional methods of learning tarot don't click with you. You also belong here if you are already a great reader but wish to be more proficient at reading tarot for others. Even professional readers will find plenty of food for thought within these pages.

This journey starts right at the beginning: What do you need to consider as you come out as a reader? How do you build fluency while also being mindful of the difference between the message and your opinion? How do you tell your Queen of Swords querent what a relationship with a Knight of Wands might be like? Is the future really the future? What about the nature of fate?

Will You Give Me a Reading? is about your journey toward querent-centered sessions where you get to decide your philosophy of reading and what that journey looks like.

There are also plenty of tarot techniques within these pages and all of it geared toward reading for others confidently and fluently. If you are an intuitive, empath, or psychic there are also techniques specifically for you (especially if you struggle with knitting your intuitive hits to the cards). You will be able to strengthen your natural talents and make them more readily available to you as a reader with some of the ideas I offer in these pages.

You get to learn all of this from a tarot reader in the trenches with you. This book is filled to the brim with personal anecdotes and stories chosen to illustrate lessons learned, and techniques that work. This means that you get a ringside seat to hands-on, immediately actionable advice, from a full-time professional reader, and teacher. You have something amazing to give, so let's hone how you give it! All levels are welcome, all that is needed is curiosity and a little magic.

1
Your Quick Start Guide to Giving a Reading

Perhaps you've agreed to give someone a reading very soon from now, and you've grabbed this book to panic-read what the hell to do. This chapter is for you. I am assuming in this guide that, on some level, you have *some* baseline familiarity of how to read tarot. By that, I am assuming that you know the following:

- Tarot is a deck of cards that have images on them.
- Those images are symbols that describe the meaning or feeling of that card.
- We use tarot to help us answer questions (even a general reading is asking a question).
- We ask a question, shuffle the deck, then choose and place specific cards in front of us.
- We read the images of each card, combining the messages of each into a story.
- That story answers the question in some way.

I intentionally did not add "memorize fifty different possible meanings for each card, and study tarot rigorously for five years, then maybe you are ready to read tarot for someone." Here's the deal, though: tarot wants to be read. Your tarot cards want you to read with them! Your deck does not want to sit on a shelf all sad and lonely while you take another year to think about how to read tarot. Tarot reading is a practice, and it is only by practicing that we become the best readers we can be. Tarot is a hands-on activity, which means you have to jump in and read in order to learn tarot, not the other way around. Studying alone won't make you a strong reader; reading is what makes you a strong reader.

Most people start their tarot journey by reading for themselves. We can get pretty far with that. But we can go farther in our tarot practice when we begin reading for others because reading for others changes your relationship to tarot. You are no longer a recipient of tarot's message, but rather become a participant in delivering a message to another person. In effect, you team up with tarot to co-create something for someone else. You start relating to tarot in a totally new way. You begin to see how tarot shows up for others in ways that are specific, unique, and totally keyed for that individual. You start to see the mastermind of tarot in ways you never could if you just read for yourself alone. Therefore, learning to read well for others makes you a better reader overall.

Now, reading for another person requires a unique set of skills and techniques. You also have a responsibility to the querent (a word meaning the person presenting the question). Sometimes that responsibility feels like it is too much. You start asking yourself questions like, "What if I am wrong? What if they get hurt? Who am I to play this role? What if they get mad at me?"

It is a lot of pressure to read for another person. It's so much pressure that some readers decide it is not worth it, and that is certainly fair. Unless you live in a shipping container out in the deep woods, though, there usually comes a time when someone you know figures out that you know your way around a tarot deck and they are going to ask, "Will you give me a reading?"

Will you say "yes"? I want you to say "yes." I hope you say "yes." And the moment you do, here is the little guide I wrote that can help you do that in a way that honors you, your querent, and this grand and beautiful act that is reading tarot.

Here is your ten-minute, quick guide to ensuring that a good time is had by all.

Don't Panic

Take a deep breath and take things one step at a time. Querents are far more forgiving and are far kinder than you are to yourself. Please remember that.

If You Have No Idea What Any Card Means

I'm not going to lie, this is not an ideal situation. But you can still work with what you've got. Here is what I recommend: look at each card and pick one symbol within that image and decide what that symbol means to you. For example, say you are looking at the High Priestess. Is there a symbol in her picture that your eyes immediately focus on? What is that symbol? How does it make you feel? What do you think it might represent? How might that symbol be part of answering the question? Start there.

You Are (Probably) Not a Mind Reader

Despite what querents might assume, you do not know what they are really thinking. Often, people believe that they shouldn't tell you "too much" in case that influences the reading. But since we are reading cards and those cards are pulled at random after a shuffle, that shouldn't matter, right? If you do not understand their question or you feel that their question is too vague, ask them to just spit it out. Help them find the question they have trouble finding within themselves.

Listen

As your querent is talking about their situation, deeply listen to them. Give them your full attention. If you are half-listening and half-thinking about the spread to use or trying to formulate their question for them, you might miss incredibly important information. Also, don't jump to conclusions about what they really want. Listen to the actual concerns they want answered.

Help Them Hone the Question

Sometimes querents come to you without a succinct question in mind. They will say something like, "I'm just open to whatever the Universe has to say to me today." While you can certainly do a general reading for them, often the cards will be speaking to so many things that none of them will carry the level of attention that will satisfy the querent. When you help them narrow their question down to once specific thing, all the cards will speak to that issue. We'll go into more depth on this topic later in the book.

Meet Them Where They Are

Each question offered by a querent resides somewhere on an axis not unlike Maslow's Hierarchy of Needs. That is, some people need to know when their extra paycheck is coming while others are asking about their karma in this lifetime. As readers, we are in service to the querent, so if they want to know about that paycheck, we read on that. If we ignore their concerns to make this a reading about something we think is "more spiritually important," we have just taken their power away from them. We always want to meet people where they are and go from there.

Don't Do Anything That Feels Icky

We may get questions that don't make us feel good as readers. We are allowed to say no. Never do a reading that conflicts with your internal moral compass. Tell them that you cannot do that question. Don't just change it on them in the middle of the reading.

Shuffling Your Deck

You can shuffle your deck, or your querent can shuffle your deck. You can cut the cards, or you can put them in a pile facedown and mix them up like dominoes. You can take one minute, or you can take five minutes. There is no hard or fast rule, here. All you need to know is that you do it until it feels right to stop. Just please don't bend your cards super hard. Not because they will get mad at you, but because this wears them out faster.

Touching the Cards

Some readers let their querents touch the deck; others do not. This is totally up to you. What I like to do is ask the querent to hold the deck while they think of their question. I do it this way because I may not like how my querents shuffle my deck, but it also gives the querent (and myself) a moment to ground and center while focusing on the question. You can do it any way that you want.

Function over Form

Once you have the question and are thinking about how to conduct the reading, ask yourself, "Does the spread I chose actually answer their question?"

For example, if they are asking about their date tonight, why would I pull a "Past, Present, Future" spread? The past and present positions may not be helpful. Make sure that the spread you are using (if any) is the right tool for the job.

Choosing the Cards

You can take a card from the top of the pile. You can take a card from a cut. You can fan out all the cards and choose one while invoking Hekate for a good reading. None of this makes a reading better than another. Do what feels right for you, understanding that the cards that are chosen are the right cards for the reading.

Read What You See

You have only one job, and that is to read the tarot. If you find yourself sharing an opinion, delving into armchair therapy, or dispensing advice, make sure that you can see it in the cards.

Just Say It

Sometimes the things you see don't make a lot of sense to you. Say them anyway. A querent may be able to connect the dots better than you as they have more information about what is going on in their lives.

Answer the Question

The cards are answering the question put forth by your querent. For example, say a querent asked whether they should buy a house, and you start talking about the psychological turmoil their teenaged daughter is having about moving. This is a deflection tactic wherein you are changing the question to fit the cards rather than seeing how the cards are answering the question (trust me, they are). There may be more information beyond the question which is good to share, but make sure that you are answering the question your querent asked, first.

If You Draw a Blank

It happens. Please refer back to tip number one: don't panic. Next, ascertain whether the question was succinct enough. Perhaps the question needs some rewording, it might need to be more specific. Then, see if the cards are only telling part of the story, and if so, draw more cards until it feels like you see a whole narrative. Finally, if nothing is working, record the reading but walk away from it right now. That is okay to do and does not mean you are a bad reader! Even the Magic 8 Ball has the "ask again later" message. Sometimes, it just isn't showing up, and that is okay.

Don't Force It

Sometimes, you cannot puzzle the meaning of a card. If you are not seeing the message, then skip that card and keep going. Don't let one card that is vexing you influence the rest of the reading.

Be Honest

If you do not see it, tell them. If you don't quite get how it all falls together, tell them. If you are unable to get the level of detail they want, tell them. Do not lean into speculation to make the reading make sense. Your querent will respect your honesty even if they aren't quite getting what they want in the way that they want it.

Second Guesses Are Usually Wrong

Your first instinct is typically the correct one. Trust it.

Don't Do Clarifying Cards

Okay, some people may disagree with me on this, but hear me out: in 99.98 percent of these situations, a clarifying card often causes more confusion than it helps. I find it better to do a mini reading with three to five cards, asking a new question around the point of confusion. The key difference here is that you don't just pull cards until it makes sense, you ask a question and do a reading specific to that question.

Don't Leave Them Hanging

Sometimes the final outcome of the reading is a cliff-hanger. Someone who gets the Tower as the last card of the spread could use a little reassurance around it. This is another time when a mini reading comes in handy. Ask a question that focuses on what will come after that point and do a three- to five-card spread to help the querent know more about that outcome.

It's Okay to Ignore Reversals

If you are not comfortable with reversals, do not read them. You will still get an accurate reading. Trust the deck to meet you where you are.

Don't Get Lost in the Details

Reading for others is a fluency activity. As long as you are getting the gist across, you are doing a good job. When you get hung up on details, you are taking yourself out of the flow. Fluency (and intuition) come from flow states, so try to stay in that place as much as possible.

Slow Down

If you find yourself talking fast or feel the querent is shooting rapid-fire questions at you, take a deep, long breath and slow things down. Just because a querent might want you to read on a hundred questions in ten minutes doesn't mean you should, even if you can.

They May Say It's Wrong

Querents are not the best judge of their own situations on the fly. They may tell you that things are wrong in the reading. If the reading is not landing, just keep moving forward, and let them know it might click for them later. It usually does.

Finish the Reading

Sometimes you might be interrupted by a querent who believes that you have answered their question and they want to go on to the next thing on their hit list. But if there is more to be said in the reading, give yourself the grace of conveying all that you see. You may say something that they will find irrelevant in the moment but will later understand how important that was.

Have a Clear Ending

When you set out to read for someone, it is often helpful to clarify how much time you have for them. Also, let querents know when it is time to wrap things up. This paces the reading in a way that helps you and gives your querent an idea of what to expect.

You Are Responsible for the Reading, Not Their Reaction

We are going to go into this at great length later on, but for now try not to take their reaction personally. People react for all sorts of reasons, and it usually has nothing to do with you.

Tarot Is Not an Analog Version of Google

The art of tarot is beautifully holistic. Even when we ask a concise question and the reading is clear, it does not mean that we are entitled to have the answer served up to us on a platter. Oracle work meanders—it is intentionally ambiguous at times and, to my mind at least, it is wonderfully mysterious in incredible ways. Often, the mystery revealed needs to be puzzled over, reflected on, or allowed to blossom slowly over time. Be gentle with yourself and remind your querent that a reading is an experience, not an analytics report.

Mutual Respect and Kind Regard

You have the right to refuse doing a reading for anyone. In fact, if someone upsets you and you still try to conduct the reading, the reading will suffer. Your hurt or even anger (or theirs) will spill out all over the reading, influencing it. Make it clear to your querents that their attitude affects the way the cards unfold and your ability to interpret them. A session is a co-creative process, and their kind reception is necessary. If you find that someone's bad behavior continues, you have every right to end the reading.

So there you have it. I hope that you are now emboldened to go out there and read your heart out. If you are new to reading for others, then welcome to the club. If you are an old hand, thank you for being here and for doing the work.

At the end of each chapter is an activity I've created that should help you deepen your tarot practice in some way as we go through the book. Below is a simple activity that I felt was a wonderful way to begin: the creation of a touchstone that acts as a "coming home" place for you no matter what you do or where you go as a tarot reader. I am so glad that you are here.

Activity
Touchstone Tarot

The touchstone is a black slab of stone that was used in ancient times to test for purity in metals such as gold. Metallurgists and merchants would take a coin or a nugget and scratch it on the touchstone. The kind of mark it left would indicate the purity of the metals in the item.

Similarly, most readers have one card in the deck that they identify with. We use that one card to determine whether we will buy or work with a given deck. While deciding on a deck, if that card does not resonate with us in a way that strikes us as true, we keep walking.

Your touchstone is the one card that speaks to you most deeply. This card acts as home base for you as you tour through the images and stories within tarot. It is the card that you will scratch all the other cards against to see how true they are. It often acts as a gateway to the various images of the deck.

Your activity is to create a mini reading using your touchstone card. You will reserve your touchstone tarot card and pull one other card from your deck to create a two-card dialogue for each question. Write the reading as if your touchstone is interacting with the other card. If you are brand new to tarot, feel free to use the book that came with your deck or any other tarot book with meanings, but also feel free to add your own meanings. Ask questions like these (an example of a mini reading follows):

★ What personal strengths do I bring to the world as I come out as a reader?

★ What limiting belief do I have that will block my capacity to emerge as a reader in the world?

★ What tools do I have that will help me make this journey as a tarot practitioner?

★ How do I let go of what people think about me being a reader?

Example

My personal touchstone card is Strength.

Question: What personal strengths do I bring to the world as I come out as I truly am?

Cards: Strength and Ace of Swords

Strength: I learned to wield power with force, loyalty, and affection. My power lies in the balance of the mind and the heart, but I also must pick up the sword. What gifts do you bring to me?

Ace of Swords: When you wield me, I add boundaries, intellect, and clear communication to your cause. Through me, you learn to speak your truth. I add precision to your world of force. The lion's teeth are a fierce thing, but my power is in cold calculation. Wield me with great care.

Your turn!

2

What Makes for a Good Reader?

There is a huge, fundamental shift that happens when we begin to read for others. We change from being the recipient of the message to the being the messenger. Once you take on that active role, you now get to peek behind the curtain, so to speak. Reading tarot this way does require a set of skills different from readings done for yourself. How well you practice those skill sets is a key factor that shapes the kind of reader you will be.

I have found that no matter where a reader is in their tarot practice, there are three foundational aspects that make good readers. In fact, many challenges I hear readers talk about usually have to do with one of these: handling criticism, engaging empathetically, and having healthy boundaries. These three skill sets define, support, and empower us as readers while providing the best possible experience for our querents.

> ### Reader's Tip
> You do not have to be a near-perfect spiritual guru on a mountaintop in order to be a good reader. You can successfully deliver amazing love readings while your own love life is in shambles. You can absolutely dispense helpful work advice while not holding down a job yourself. Your personal perfection as a human being has no bearing whatsoever on your skill as a reader.

Dealing with Criticism

I remember my first public tarot reading event like it was yesterday. It isn't a memory one could forget. On my neighborhood block, I had the incredible luck of having two houses owned by men who were active in the local drag queen scene, and they knew how to throw a party.

One of those men bought me my first deck, and it was these two men who invited me to read tarot at their Halloween Victor/Victoria party. Too young to be self-conscious, I dressed up and headed over to find a lovely little table waiting for me. I remember spending hours glued to the seat at my table as I read for all kinds of people: gorgeous queens, handsome kings, men and women of all walks of life. Grown adults were giving me the time of day! I felt important and heard. Folks, I had arrived!

I'm sure I made so many mistakes that night such as taking way too long for some readings and not long enough for others. I am totally sure I stumbled through the deck as I read, but at no point did anyone make me feel bad or get frustrated with me. In fact, I was heartily encouraged to keep it up by everyone. It could not have been a better "coming out of the tarot box" experience, and that experience has deeply shaped how I read today, many decades later.

While not everyone gets their own troop of local drag queens to cheer us on, each one of us has a coming-out story. Maybe that story is yet to be as you are contemplating how to go public and for others it has happened, already. Whether those stories were joyous or strained, your coming out of the tarot box story has a key role in shaping the kind of tarot practitioner you are.

For some readers, a coming-out story can be fraught with difficulty. Perhaps you live in a community or come from a family of origin that takes a dim view on tarot or you have a career that would roast you should it be known that you pull a few cards. These kinds of circumstances certainly make it harder to read for others because coming out can have real consequences.

Personally, it was when I went professional that I had the hardest time. I was terrified of my old colleagues and work buddies finding out. I was scared that they would think that I was not intelligent or that I had completely lost my rocker. This was hard because I have a deep need to be seen as competent. It crushed me to think that my intelligence, value, and worth as a person might take a nosedive just because I read tarot.

I am happy to report, however, that most of my fears were never realized. My life has only gotten better, brighter, wiser, and more complete because of the role tarot has had in my life. I get to share that with others who understand (like you!). But these fears can keep us from living our lives as authentically as we would like. So, the first part of being a good tarot reader is figuring out how to handle judgment and criticism.

Often, we respond to criticism according to our own deeply embedded way of handling trauma. Some of us are going to *fight*: the fighters will push back and not be afraid of confrontation. Others will deploy *flight*: preferring to only read where they know they will have a receptive audience or otherwise avoiding any uncomfortable feelings entirely. Those whose trauma response is *freeze* may stop reading tarot altogether, while those who take a *fawn* approach will turn themselves into pretzels to make everyone happy. Most of us will tend toward one reaction most strongly, but all of these responses could be present. When judgement or criticism rears its head, we can change our response to it by replacing trauma-learned reactions with healthy ones.

The following activity may help you shift your trigger response. Take out the four Knights from your tarot deck and turn them so that they are reversed with their heads facing down. Each reversed Knight corresponds to a trauma response:

- Knight of Wands = Flight
- Knight of Swords = Fight
- Knight of Cups = Fawn
- Knight of Pentacles = Freeze

Think about your go-to trigger response and pull that Knight aside. Next, take out only the court cards from your deck and add the remaining three Knights into that pile. Now think about your own trigger response: your Knight reversed. Ask yourself: what other court card might help this Knight respond more healthfully? If you have little experience with the court cards, look at the images of each of the court cards and choose the one that feels relieving or safe for you. Or you might shuffle the court cards and pull one at random. How you decide to choose the second court card is up to you.

The second court card represents a healthy aspect of you that needs to be integrated. That is, this healthy part of you can serve as the brakes to slow down the runaway Knight that triggered you. Here is an example:

Knight of Pentacles (reversed) and Page of Swords

Let's say that when I get triggered, I am the type to freeze up. No matter how much I tell myself to do something, I just don't. I get stuck and seem unable to progress. I am like a turtle in my shell.

I chose the Page of Swords as the healthy aspect because, to me, this Page represents curiosity. I cannot force myself to come out of my shell, but I can use the gift of curiosity which engages my positive feelings and helps remind me that I have free will in my situation. When I am curious, I stay out of judgement mode by looking at the facts of the situation at hand while asking, "Why is that?"

Reminding ourselves of our innate healthy aspects helps to de-escalate the volume of a triggered response. It also lets the part of ourselves that feels unsafe know that they are loved and supported. You can even say something like, "Thank you, reversed Knight, for trying so hard to protect me. But I got this; you can relax. See, we have the Page who is also going to help us."

Trauma responses never disappear if we try to shove them down or become angry with ourselves for having them. The only way forward is to love them. It is only when those aspects of ourselves feel safe and cared for that they begin to dissipate. And handling our triggers is only half of the story here. The other half is what to do with the information that triggered us in the first place. First, we see if the criticism has any merit. If it does, we see how we might make it better for the person with the criticism, or we explore how we can become better for others moving forward. A good question to ask yourself is this, "What am I actually responsible for?"

Receiving judgment from people about you reading tarot or criticism about how you read tarot is never easy. You are being tasked with an incredible challenge: seeing what is yours to fix while also not spiraling into defensiveness, owning what is yours to handle while ignoring biased opinions, and holding space for querents who may not be able to do the same for you. But I believe that you are here reading this because the Universe has an invitation for you. Those of us who are chosen for this work are not chosen because we like things easy. In fact, we are called to this work because we are helpers, and, as they say, "look to the helpers." I am looking right at you!

Practicing Empathy

Let me lay out an important distinction. Empathy is a skill distinct from being an empath. (Confusing, I know, as the words are so closely linked.) An empath is someone who can feel the emotions of another person, an ability can take on an extra-sensory type of sensitivity, wherein an empath absorbs and feels the feeling of another person.

Empaths typically struggle to learn how to create distance between other people's emotions and their own. As a tarot reader, being an empath makes your work harder—taking on a querent's emotions could actively influence the reading. In my experience (discussed later in chapter 2, "What Makes for a Good Reader?"), strong emotions hinder the clarity of a reading. Empaths need a lot of grounding, shielding, and training to contain their natural talent when it comes to reading tarot for others. I offer resources in chapter 2 to help if this is something you struggle with, too.

In contrast, empathy is a person's ability to put themselves in the shoes of another. It is a cognitive skill that is partly inherited but can also be trained. Empathy allows us to imagine what someone else is going through and allows us to feel for someone but not take on their feelings, per se. With empathy, you feel *for* someone. As an empath you feel *as* someone. They seem similar, but the difference is huge.

"Empathy" and "empath" are not interchangeable terms, and in fact, being an empath does not guarantee having empathy. I've seen tarot readers say things like, "When she came for a reading, I was overcome with a dread and deep depression. I felt suicidal, and it was so intense. I just couldn't take her energy." This tarot reader is an empath, no doubt. But the focus is not on how she felt as a result of interacting with the querent. It stopped being about the querent and became about the reader.

If that same querent came to a reader who was practicing empathy, she might have said instead, "My querent's head was hanging low, and her feet shuffled as she walked in. It was obvious that she was in a place of deep pain. She told me about her economic troubles, and I could just imagine how hard it has been for her and her family. My stomach is tight just thinking about her situation."

Practicing empathy is a skill a good tarot reader needs. In fact, it is empathy that can fundamentally make or break a session. Even if you are not so good with your cards just yet, the practice of empathy with querents will make up for that. Everyone wants to be seen and understood. One of your roles as a reader is to show querents that they are seen and understood with your presence and your actions.

To prove my point, I recently pulled my reviews from querents over the years to see what they said about me and if there were any commonalities in their experiences. I was surprised to discover that they actually rarely talked about the reading; how skillful it was, how accurate, or even how helpful. What my querents mostly talked about was how they *felt* as a result of spending time with me. This was a huge revelation.

Reader's Tip

Feelings will not tell us how accurate we are or how masterfully we executed the reading. Feelings tell us how we *deliver* the reading. Querents will not remember every line item of what the reading entailed, but they will remember how they *felt*.

As you think about your reading practice, consider how you want your querents to feel. What do you wish more than anything for your querent to experience with you? Where do you sit on the spectrum between "truth at any cost" to "feeling good no matter what" when working with querents?

Want to do a little empathy practice with me? It starts with pulling a card. Choose a card that is negative or difficult, where it is clear that the person in the image is having a tough time. Take a card and look at the image. What is going on for this person? What are they feeling? What do they need? How might a reading help them? How would you help them?

Now look through the rest of the cards and choose one that looks helpful. Imagine that helpful card doing its work for that person. Finally, look for a final card that shows the person in a better place as a result of the supporting card. How do they look now? How are they feeling? How did your help get them to that better place? As an example, I chose Four of Pentacles for the person in need of help, Six of Cups for the helping card, and the Chariot for the card that shows them in a better place.

Four of Pentacles, Six of Cups, and the Chariot

Four of Pentacles: The person in the image looks isolated. They may feel defensive and that they cannot trust anyone. Perhaps they have been treated badly and now feel like the world is an unsafe place. They look stuck in this place, trying to hold on to what they have. Perhaps they need a reading to give them hope, to remind them that the world is full of good, too.

Six of Cups: This card shows an offering made from one person to another. The scene feels gentle, kind, and helpful. Perhaps this is someone showing up to remind the hurting person that they are deserving of care and that it is okay to accept help and support.

The Chariot: As a result of this support, our person finds it within themselves to let go of holding on to all those coins. Instead of feeling stuck, they are open, strong, and moving into a new direction with a focus on where they are going rather than on what has happened.

Empathy is one of the critical skills that sets good readers apart from the rest. The capacity to hold space for your querents is an act of service. Empathy centers the reading on the querent and makes every moment about them. Empathy is a critical factor to helping us "step out of the way" to better play the role of messenger. Rather than sugarcoat a reading to make the reading look good so the querent is happy, empathy is about ensuring that the querent feels cared for, whether in a ten-minute reading or an hour-long session.

Honoring Boundaries

The third most important skill a good tarot reader needs is establishing boundaries. Much of the anguish or confusion a reader encounters is due to a lack of boundaries with either the querent or within themselves. Boundaries work is critical but is often so hard for us readers to enforce.

Readers are typically the type of people who just want to make the world better in some way. The nicest people you will ever meet are readers; their capacity to care is so huge! That caring nature is an incredible gift to the world. But givers and carers typically struggle with enacting and enforcing boundaries. It can feel so alien. I mean, how are we caring for someone while saying no? Readers often find it unnatural.

The reason for this cognitive dissonance is that many people who are drawn to reading tarot are also the type of people who learned from family and society that their worth is only derived from their capacity to give. So if a reader draws a boundary, they can feel like they are not giving, and if they are not giving, maybe they aren't worth so much. For many, to draw a boundary is a trigger right into the heart of the most deeply-held beliefs. It is a tough nut to crack.

Boundaries work is also hard because we might be scared of making someone angry or hurting their feelings. We may hope that they take the hint and act accordingly, but that rarely works—instead, we need to use our words. We need to communicate our needs clearly. If they respond in a negative way, we honor our own boundaries with ourselves. *Their reaction is not our responsibility*. It is incredibly hard, no doubt about that. But your work with boundaries is absolutely necessary to ensure that you are living within your values and truth while honoring others, difficult as it may be. It is true that in some ways, it is easier to be a doormat, but that's just a different kind of hard, isn't it?

This topic reminds me of a situation that happened while I was writing this book. I did a gallery style reading (reading with a mic for a crowd) at a public venue. At the start of the night, I told everyone that I would not do readings on death, divorce, or disease but everything else was fine. The attendees wrote their questions on slips of paper and put them in a glass bowl next to me. The gallery was going great until I got a slip that asked, "My dad left my mom when they were still pretty young. I'm now at the age my mom was when he divorced her. So, when is my husband going to divorce me?"

There was no discernable way I could spin this question for a public reading, so I had to—as compassionately as I could—tell her that I could not answer that question. I asked if she had another question she wanted to ask; she did not. I told her to see me personally after the show so we could talk at length later.

Instead of coming up to me after the event, she sat at her table shooting daggers at me with her eyes. She chose not to engage within the space I offered. I still occasionally see her whenever I am in that town, and it is eye-daggers every time. Let me tell you, it is not fun. A younger me would have seen her reaction as an indictment on me as a reader. I would have beaten myself up wondering if there was a better way to handle the situation and obsessing over her dislike of me. Due to my work with boundaries, empathy, and managing my reaction to criticism, however, I was able to manage this moment more healthfully. I could understand that her reaction came from a place of deep pain. To her, my boundary may have felt like public rejection. I bet our interaction triggered something within her that fueled her anger. It didn't mean that my boundary was wrong; it didn't mean that I am bad. It only meant that she reacted to it negatively, and her reactions are not my responsibility. I could hold my boundaries while simultaneously empathizing with her pain and rejecting the criticism that came along with it. Yay for me!

Your boundaries are yours alone, and they are sacred. They will be unique to you, and you don't owe anyone an explanation for them. You may not even know that you have a boundary until it has been crossed. As you become more public with your readings, you will have situations that will be lessons in your boundary work.

Recently, I was shopping for a dress. As the assistant was ringing me up, I said that I was looking for a specific outfit for work. She asked me what I did, and I told her, "I am a professional intuitive." Without skipping a beat, she said, "Well, what do you see about me?" Not even a "please" came with that demand!

I responded, "Are you going to give me a discount for giving you a reading?" She drew back, offended, but I meant it. That was my boundary. Just because someone knows I am a reader does not mean that I am obligated to read for anyone.

Looking back over the years, I cannot recall one instance where I broke my own boundary that made me feel better. In fact, I look back, and I want to grab my own hand and say, "Darling, love yourself enough to say no."

Here are some of the questions that I think about and, honestly, regret the ways I did not honor my own boundaries: Why did I answer my phone at ten o'clock at night for a querent? Why did I do a reading on my day off? Why did I say yes to work for "exposure"? Why did I read for a friend and her troublesome boyfriend knowing it was going to bite me in the ass? Why did I ask about a situation over a friendly phone call, putting myself right back into reader mode? Why did I agree to read for someone when I was on a new migraine medication and could barely keep my head up?

What are you responsible for, really? What are your agreements to yourself and others as a tarot reader? Below are some boundaries to help you in your practice. If reading them makes you feel uncomfortable or worried, then that is a key area where you need to do the self-love task of saying "no" more often.

Common Boundaries for Tarot Readers

You are not obliged to:

- tell people you read tarot, even if they ask
- prove yourself or pass "tests" of your skills and capabilities
- read tarot how *they* want you to if you do it differently
- read for someone just because they know you read tarot
- read for every question and circumstance
- use tarot to make someone feel better
- be available for readings whenever they want one
- read tarot if you don't feel like it
- read for exposure
- keep reading past the time you had available because a querent wants more
- fix someone's problem
- be 100 percent accurate or 100 percent clear
- change a reading (or add to a reading) to please a querent

When we do not honor our own boundaries, resentment can set in. When we hold resentment, we get in the way of the reading. In our desire to do something to make someone else happy at the cost of our own well-being, we decrease our capacity to be the best reader we can be.

A key aspect to boundaries is managing our own guilt when we deploy them. Luckily, we have a great tool (seventy-eight tools, in fact) that can help us heal our relationship to guilt so that it is no longer a factor when stating our boundaries. Look through your deck and pick a card that feels like obligation to you. If you do not know tarot yet, just choose an image that feels right to you. Here I have chosen the Ten of Wands:

Ten of Wands

As you look at your card of obligation, I invite you to feel the emotion of guilt. Ask yourself where this guilt is coming from. What is the first memory that comes to mind? Choose a card to represent that. For me, that would be the Five of Pentacles:

Five of Pentacles

As you think of your card that represents a deep memory or belief (for me, the Five of Pentacles represents an underlying belief that if I was not doing everything for everyone, then maybe I was not worth very much or would not be accepted.) Think about what this card needs in order to be healed. For me, I chose the Ace of Cups, the card of love.

Ace of Cups

Looking at these cards, I understand that when I am able to fill my cup first and love myself fully and completely, then the only person I need to prove my worth to is myself. I imagine swimming in a big cup full of warm water, filled with love and acceptance. When I am enough for myself, the guilt of saying "no" falls away. I do not have to prove my value to anyone.

The skills of managing criticism well, holding empathy for others, and maintaining boundaries are foundational aspects to reading with confidence (in addition to reading tarot well, of course). Confidence acts as a feedback loop that only enhances and increases our skill as readers while also being of service to our querents in kind and helpful ways. Confidence is the outward expression of wisdom in action. When you are confident, your readings will reflect that clarity, too.

Activity
Practicing Empathy

Empathy is a surprisingly uncommon skillset and is typically not one people are taught. The good news is that it can be learned, and when you do it well, your readings will massively benefit. You start with these four easy steps:

1. Listen with curiosity.
2. Validate their emotions.
3. Conduct the reading.
4. Validate again as you sum up the message.

Step 1: Listen with Curiosity

As your querent is talking about why they would like a reading, give them your full attention while also asking follow-up questions to indicate that you care about them and their situation. Look at their body language or their general vibe. What emotions are you getting from this person? Imagine how you would feel if you were in their shoes, and let them know you care. Do not give advice at this point. Right now you're holding space for someone, and it is a *huge* deal.

Step 2: Validate Their Emotions

You can go a long way with someone by indicating that how they feel is valid. It's not the same as agreeing with them or telling them that they are right—rather, you are showing them that you understand how they feel. As you are listening, choose one emotion that seems particularly relevant and mention it.

Step 3: Conduct the Reading

Now step aside and let tarot do its thing. The reading will know what to say, and the querent will be more likely to be open to the reading because you have done the prep work in helping them feel heard and safe. Never sugarcoat the reading. That is, never make it sound more positive than it is. Sugarcoating a reading is codependent behavior—the urge to insulate someone from a reading that makes them feel bad. When we do that, we are no longer messengers.

Step 4: Validate Their Feelings as You Sum Up the Message

Once again, show them that you understand how they feel. Validate their vulnerability by thanking them for sharing with you.

Your activity for this chapter is to imagine four different kinds of people to read for and use the four-step method to read empathetically for them. Use a spread depending on your skill level. If you are new, pull one card. If you know how to read more fluently, pull three cards. Here are your scenarios:

1. A friend or close family member lost their job. When will they get a new one?
2. A neighbor's partner was arrested for driving while under the influence. Will the sentence be very bad?
3. An abusive family member, someone you intensely dislike or even fear, has come down with some serious financial trouble. Will they lose the house?
4. Your best friend is cheating on their partner (whom you also love). Could their marriage be saved?

Example

Querent: "I was fooling around online, and six months later I find myself in an emotional affair with a person I've never met. I cannot believe I did that. The worst part is that my boyfriend has no idea."

Reader: "It sounds like you are in a really tough situation. What do you think would happen if your boyfriend found out?"

Querent: "I don't know! I am terrified that he will. I love him so much, but I've been so lonely since he has been working in another state. I didn't mean to fall for some rando online."

Reader: "I totally get that loneliness can make us vulnerable to things we wouldn't do otherwise—it happens! Out of this situation, what is the question that feels most important to you, right now?"

Querent: "Well, I know I want to end the emotional affair. I would like to tell my boyfriend about it, but I am scared that he will break up with me if I do. So, I guess we could ask, 'How will things go with my boyfriend if I tell him about the emotional affair?'"

Reader pulls three cards:

Five of Cups, Two of Pentacles, and Three of Wands

Reader: "He is going to be emotionally very hurt. At first, it does not look great, to be honest with you. The Five of Cups can indicate grief. But the Two of Pentacles seems to indicate that it is not over between the two of you. There could be a time where things may feel touch and go between you as you continue to navigate this challenge. Finally, the Three of Wands is often a card associated with new opportunities. It indicates that it's possible to repair the rift between you, but it will take a lot of time and effort."

Querent: "Okay, so it isn't as bad as I was imagining, then?"

Reader: "Well, it is pretty bad. The Five of Cups indicates that you two will be closer to breaking up than to staying. But the story is not over, necessarily. I know that you feel awful about what happened and that means you care about your boyfriend and you don't wish to hurt him. This is a good place to start when you tell him, you know?"

Querent: "Yes, you're right. I need to talk to him after this session."

Reader: "I can see how hard this will be for you, and that you are going to do the hard thing because you care about him so much. Thank you so much for walking through your situation with me. Now, would you like to do a follow-up reading asking, 'How should I best disclose my emotional affair to my boyfriend?' Advice on how to navigate this next step could be really useful."

Querent: "That sounds perfect. And thank you."

3
Yes, You're Psychic

Years ago, I had an apartment in a rather rough area of town. After living there for a year without any issues, I kept getting this intense feeling of being watched. I couldn't shake it. I felt unsafe but had no discernible reason for why I was feeling such discomfort. I did not see anyone watching me or my place, but it unnerved me so much that I called the police and told them that I felt that my home was being cased. They said that they would increase patrols in the area.

Two days later after returning home from work, I just *knew*. Instead of reaching for my key to unlock the deadbolt, I pushed the door and it opened right up. Once open, I could see that it had been pried open with a crowbar. I walked in to see my home completely torn apart. Books were flung from shelves. My mattress was pushed off its box spring. They were thorough. They took my grandmother's ring, my devices, anything that was worth anything. It was terrifying. In a panic, I ran out of the apartment to call the police.

My psychic abilities kicked in days before, trying to keep me safe. This is the first rule of psychic impressions: they are an evolutionary adaptation for survival. In crime stories, we hear about people suddenly hearing voices or seeing visions that save their lives just in time. This is their psychic senses jumping into action. Ask most people in private, and they will tell you about an experience they cannot explain. Extra sensory perception is something we all have, to some extent. Moreover, it is a skill that can be trained and strengthened.

While it is true that there are many tarot readers who are not psychic, I would guess that a far larger number are. If you don't feel you have or are interested in being a psychic, go ahead and skip this chapter. But if you know you are, maybe I can help you define, strengthen, and focus it while getting rid of what doesn't work or feel right for you.

Misconceptions about Being Psychic

First we have to debunk what is often considered common knowledge about what being psychic means. These are important things to understand because people will make assumptions about you and have expectations that may have no actual basis in reality. There are a couple of big misconceptions out there; here are the ones that I most commonly run across.

Being Psychic Is Not a Lifestyle Choice

If you look online, you will find articles that attempt to attribute the capacity for psychic ability with a certain "clean" lifestyle. This is just not true. You don't need to drink crystal-infused kombucha made with locally sourced honey. You don't need to do yoga every day. You don't need to meditate or pray or have an altar you visit every full moon. In fact, some of the best psychics I know are chain-smoking whiskey-drinkers. Psychic cognition is simply an ability, and it is not necessarily tied to a spiritual belief, either. You can be an atheist and psychic.

Psychic Abilities Are Morally Neutral

Being a good person doesn't mean that you will be a better psychic. You can be a terrible person and still be psychic. In fact, some con artists out there are wonderfully psychic—they use their intuitive skills to wow a mark, then move into the con part. They can discern that you have three kids and also tell you to buy a candle to remove your curse for $500. Because the first thing they said was true, many will believe the second part is true, too. As much as I would like it to be true, being psychic is not bestowed only upon the worthy. Like doing algebra, singing, or being athletic, being psychic is a skill not tied to personality or ethics.

Psychic Doesn't Mean Mind Reader

As a psychic, I get impressions, names, video feed-like messages, and just a knowing feeling. This is not the same as me reading someone's mind. I have no idea what you are thinking. A dossier of your life to the smallest details is not being downloaded into my head the moment we meet.

Being Psychic is a Selective Focus Skill Just Like Other Senses

My psychic cognition is selective. This means that I have to be actively paying attention in order to use it most of the time. Sometimes when something is particularly dangerous or important to know, I will get information (like my house being broken into). But usually it is just humming in the background below my conscious awareness. Our brains are constantly filtering out information, determining what is relevant and what is not before we are even aware of it. We only notice about 10 percent of the raw feed coming into our brains. Our minds are very good at deciding what to pay attention to, and this includes psychic information.

Reader's Tip

Communicate clearly to your querents what being psychic means for you, not what they think it should mean for you. Ultimately, you get to decide whether you want to even use the word "psychic" (as it is a heavily loaded term), "intuitive," or nothing at all. Perhaps you will keep your psychic skills secret as you tell your querents that it is just the cards. There is no wrong or right answer, and your approach may change as you deepen in your tarot practice. This is all okay!

What Does a Psychic Impression Feel Like?

Now that we have talked about the experience of being psychic in the world, let's shift gears and explore what being psychic actually means, and feels like. Once you begin to recognize a psychic hit when it comes, it will be easier to sense what is from a non-ordinary source, and what is just speculation. I made a silly little acronym for psychic impressions: FUMI—fast, unemotional, multiple impressions.

Fast

If you have ever watched a psychic or medium work whether on TV or in person, you might have noticed that they usually talk fast. This is because psychic impressions are quick. The trick is to grab that initial hit before you lose it. The impression gets lost if not caught quickly.

An analogy I use for this phenomenon is called the fish and the wave. Your psychic hit is that quick little fish darting about below the waves at the edge of the ocean. Your job is to bend down and pick up that fish before the tsunami (composed of your logic, objections, judgments, and insecurities) comes crashing down on the both of you. Once the wave crashes, the fish is gone. Since you have been trained to think logically and cogently, this kind of trust with a gut instinct is initially hard to have. But you can do things to retrain your brain to recognize and amplify the psychic hit.

One of the most powerful ways to train your mind is improv. Yes, improv! Live improv classes force you to learn how to grab the first thing that comes to mind and run with it. You don't have time to think, overthink, or strategize a different response. This is an amazing skill set that will amplify your capacity to hear and relay your impressions. Besides improv, any game that forces you to think fast will also help, such as Taboo or even Pictionary. Automatic writing is also a technique that can help you learn to transmit your impressions without judging or changing them in any way.

Reader's Tip

It was no accident my first book, *Have Tarot Will Travel*, was about how to do festival-based tarot readings as a pro. Gig work forces a reader to spit out psychic impressions in rapid-fire, one after the other. The time constraint forces you to embrace the fast context of psychic hits. I truly believe a reader who does five festivals within a few months will become a much stronger reader than the one who just does emailed readings for years. Even if you are not a pro reader, you can recreate a situation like this for friends and family. When you only have ten minutes with the querent, you don't have time to overthink anything; overthinking is the tsunami, the enemy of psychic impressions.

Unemotional

Okay, here is my caveat: if you are empathic this may not be true for you. But in general, psychic impressions lack emotion. Those powerful insights like, "He has cancer" are loud in a way that compels me to blurt them out, but it is not accompanied by fear or worry, it is just the information. Now, I may have an emotional reaction afterward, but that emotion is a response to the information that is transmitted.

Sometimes you will get a sense that something is not right that also feels emotionally uncomfortable. That "I've got a funny feeling about this" is often intuition (unconscious knowledge trying to make itself known) which is totally valid, and you should trust it. However, it might be nothing more than your worry or anxiety that has no basis in anything. The more you train yourself, the easier it will be to ascertain which is which.

Multiple Impressions

I think one of my pet peeves is the overidentification with which "clair" are you? Are you clairaudient? How about clairvoyant? Maybe you are clairsentient? Psychic cognition, while very natural, doesn't work at all like the other five senses but it seems that we want to shoehorn this ability into five slots anyway. If you think you are just one type, you may dismiss another way the information is trying to come through. As your ability shifts and grows, how it works for you will grow, too.

For instance, is there such a thing as clairliterate? Because when a psychic impression hits, I sometimes see an invisible hand write a word in the air. The word may change in font and color depending on the tone or feeling of the information. For example, I had a querent sit for a reading, and as soon as she did, I got a feeling for her daughter and saw the words "CAR ACCI-DENT" written in bright, red letters. I asked her to immediately call her daughter, and she did. Her daughter had just been involved in a multiple-car crash, but she was okay enough to answer the phone.

Other times I get impressions that are static images, or a brief ten-second video feed of a scene. Rarely, I will get a smell, and it is so fun when that happens! Often the impression is just knowing something; there is no associated image, sound, or word. It is just something that, all the sudden, I know is true. Other times I will hear a voice shout my name, or the name of the querent.

Even though I don't label myself explicitly as a pet psychic, a medium, a medical intuitive, or as someone who is capable of psychometry (touching things and getting impressions), these are all things I am capable of doing that can be enhanced or left alone. (You should have seen the face of the woman whose dad's graduation ring made me exclaim the name "William." I was just as surprised as she was!)

Reader's Tip

Don't worry too much about what kind of psychic you are. Focus more on sensing what you get and getting better at transmitting it. As you get stronger, you will surprise yourself by what you can do.

And that, folks, is the gist of it! In my experience, explaining psychic phenomena is fairly easy to grasp, but it is in the practice that it becomes difficult. We can all remember countless times when our gut was going off, we ignored it, and that innate sense was totally right. But if we can remember FUMI—impressions are fast (better catch them), unemotional (it is a transmission of information), and can come through as multiple impressions (be open to getting all kinds of information)—we can practice working with our psychic hits.

Receiving impressions is only half the battle because you as a reader have two modes: input (receiving the information) and output (delivering that information). Now, a lot can happen between input and output that can mess things up. The last thing we want to do is to be like Cassandra, the psychic whose messages were so cryptic that no one could use them. What good is that? The hard work of perception is only half of it, the other half is how we interpret that information and share it with others in the most accurate way possible. Below are some thoughts about what to do with those psychic downloads once you get them.

Describe What You See

We may receive information that is accurate, but we may not have the context to understand its meaning. When we aren't privy to granular details, we may attempt to fill in the gaps. This is totally normal human behavior. We love crafting meaning where there is none. Speculations can be dangerous, though, so make it clear to your querent when you are switching from psychic to logic mode.

For example, a few years ago, my father-in-law had terminal lung cancer. During the summer I got a strong impression. I had a vision of a lot of snow outside his retirement community, and, in that impression, I knew he had passed. Understandably, I told my husband that we had about six months (thinking his father had until February or March). I was wrong. My father-in-law passed on Thanksgiving Day. That year, we had an unseasonable snowstorm the night before he left us. So, my psychic impression was accurate, but I came to the wrong conclusion.

It is hard to merely describe an impression that feels incomplete. This is especially true when we read for others because our querents want more details than we might have. They might push us for more information, and it is hard not to buckle under that kind of pressure. Just describe what you see. Trust that.

Your querent will also try to close the gap by speculating where the reading is not explicitly clear. But, if they are quick to make up a definitive answer when the answer is not yet clear, they may be misled by the reading. Don't let the querents help in this way. "Oh, I know who that Knight of Cups is. He is that dude I dated last year." Unless you really sense that, don't let them come to a conclusion, even if it feels good for them to do so. You can respond with, "Maybe. But since I do not exactly see that, this could mean someone else, too. Let's stay open to that possibility."

Reader's Tip

When pressed for more detail, be honest and say you do not know. We don't have control over how information comes to us. Though your querent might want you to tell them the ID number, blood type, and address of their future husband, that doesn't mean that they're going to get it. Psychic readings can be a great help, but information comes through as it will. That is the nature of divination—we don't get to dictate how the answer wants to appear.

Don't Filter What You Get

Some of my biggest psychic hits don't make any sense. I have learned to just blurt it out, as crazy as it might sound. It is not my job to be the arbiter of what gets passed along. I am only a messenger, and when I start forgetting that fact my sessions go south pretty fast.

When I begin a sentence with, "Look, this might sound crazy and totally out of left field, but…" nine times out of ten, it is right. I had a woman in her early forties sit for a reading. She was fit, and it was obvious that she took care of her health. All of the sudden I got an image of her hips with smoke around them. (I have learned that when I see smoke or blurriness over a body part, it usually indicates a problem in that area.) This did not make sense to me. Why would a reasonably young woman have hip issues?

So, I said to her, "I know that this might sound really out there, but I keep being shown your hips. Do you have any known problems with them?" Her reaction showed the accuracy of the impression. "Yes, I am a marathon runner and have worn out my hips. I have already replaced one, and I am about to schedule replacing the other."

If I let my logical mind dictate the session, I would have just ignored this impression. I have learned to just blurt out what I see whether it makes sense to me (or them) or not. It is okay if they also cannot immediately connect the dots. It might become clear for them later on.

Read When You Feel Bad

Now, I know this sounds counterintuitive, but illness and exhaustion can sometimes help with the psychic part. Not feeling well seems to make it easier to accept the psychic hits coming through. When we feel less than our best it can actually quiet the logical mind, making it easier to pick up the impressions underneath.

Reader's Tip
Do readings at three o'clock in the morning, see what happens.

Tying Tarot and Psychic Impressions Together

I was psychic long before I learned tarot. In fact, I struggled to get my psychic ability to accept and use tarot as a tool. It took quite a while and some effort before I was getting impressions also within the cards. But once it knit together (for lack of a better term), it was an additional way that I could get information.

Use the Art of Soft Focus

I cannot overstate the importance of soft focus as an intuitive reader. Let's say that we have a question in hand and begin laying out our cards. Typically, we dive right in to immediately piece together the message. This is what I would call hard focus, but the harder our focus is, the narrower our field of vision gets. Soft focus is the art of letting your peripheral vision take over and let your gaze soften. With soft focus, our field of vision is wider, it is more like a gentle awareness than a scan.

I realized this trick when I started to learn how to forage for mushrooms and woodland edibles. I noticed that a hard focus in the woods isn't helpful, there are too many things to look at. But, when I stopped trying so hard and let a softer gaze and awareness settle in, I would find things more successfully.

So, when you lay out your cards give it a minute and try not to look too hard at anything. Does anything arise? Do you get the sense of information somehow "between" the cards? Does a truth come to you that you know is tarot-informed, but you cannot exactly pinpoint how you got there? That is usually soft focus in action.

Notice Where Your Eyes Wander

One of the ways that my clairvoyance uses the symbology of tarot is that it gets me to notice things within the tarot image that I usually don't. If I find myself focused on an image within a card this is usually a sign that my clairvoyance is using the symbol to get my logical mind to know something. Noticing what I notice as I look at cards is a fundamental tip; my intuition is lifting certain symbols out of the many and the reason why is typically important.

A particularly good example of this comes from the time I was reading at the opening of a large department store. I had a young woman sit down and ask me, "How is my boyfriend?" It was as vague a question as one can get. At the time, I was reading with Robert Place's Alchemical Tarot. In it, his Eight of Swords depicts an animal who is manacled by one leg and he is shackled to the ground. My eyes felt compelled to notice the shackle. Normally, it is not an aspect of the card in this deck that I pay attention to, but I could not avert my eyes from it. I knew that the symbol in that image was trying to tell me something.

I kept asking myself, "What are you telling me?" Then it hit me like a bolt of lightning. This young man was in jail. So, I asked her, "Is your boyfriend incarcerated?"

She said, "Yes."

Building Your Personal Lexicon

Psychics usually have a lexicon, an internal symbols dictionary, that their psychic aspect uses to key their logical minds. For example, a psychic may know that the person showing up in her mind's eye has passed on because it shows up on the left side of her. Over time, we will begin to use the imagery within the tarot to add to that private lexicon and it may have nothing to do with the traditional meaning of the card.

For example, the Ten of Swords is often a "back surgery" card for me, and the Five of Swords is my ultimate "got the job" card. Don't stress if you find that what works for you doesn't match what the books say. Personally, I use both intuitive hits and standard meanings. I toggle back and forth between those to build a narrative. Why choose only one? Why not use every tool in the toolbox?

Reader's Tip

Some people are "no tools psychics" and while what they do is amazing, a psychic who uses a medium is just as incredible. You may encounter an unfortunate, yet common, perception that using "no tools" means that the psychic is better. However, that is not a good measurement of psychic ability. A better measurement is in the proof of service. Were they accurate, was it helpful, was it a special experience? This is what matters, no matter how a psychic gets there. So, if you use tarot or runes or chicken bones thrown on the floor, that is your special magic, and you are just as good as anyone else!

Activity
Tarot in the World

As we build our relationship to tarot as psychic readers or build our psychic skills as tarot readers, we come to understand that tarot is more than just a deck of cards. Tarot is greater than the static, symbolic imagery it represents. The Sun, the Moon, the Star—tarot is representative of the world we encounter, but what's really cool about it is that it is also representative of the mysterious. Tarot is the bridge between the ordinary world and the non-ordinary world of spirit. Tarot can be the scaffolding upon which you build your own capacity to perceive information from nontraditional sources.

Over time, you may find that you will be able to do tarot readings without a deck at all. As you cast your question into the winds, you will notice imagery in the world that will be the reading. Your lexicon will leap off the cards and in the world around you—all without engaging your logical mind or straining for it.

Notice tarot in the world around you. For a week or so, every day, pick a card from your deck and tell yourself that you are now looking for examples of that image in the world. It can be something visual or even words. If, for example, you drew Death, you probably won't see a dude in a cowl (or maybe you will!), but you might see that your eye is drawn to that word, or to the color black. It will come in strange or unexpected ways.

At the end of each day, record your findings. Maybe nothing came to you. That is fine; it doesn't mean you have failed this activity. Part of the learning goal for this activity is to recognize when you are reaching and grasping and engaging your logical mind—and letting it go. The symbol will come through when it needs to. You are training your mind to be able to use anything as a key for information.

Your Life is a Spread

Once you start to intuitively see tarot in the world, see if you can create a three-card spread of your day. Ask the Universe a question. For example, "Will I get the house I just bid on?" and see if you get three images through your day that answer that. Maybe in the morning you notice your change sitting on the dresser and count it out to find six coins. The Six of Pentacles is your first one. Then over lunch you notice four chopsticks laid out on the table. Great, there's your Four of Wands! Finally, late that night you watch a movie and notice that it is about a drag race. There is your Chariot!

While this activity seems easy to do, it is incredibly hard to pull off. You will have to fight your natural tendency to make this a logic game. Remember FUMI: fast, unemotional, multiple impressions. Ask the question and try to forget about it during the day. The answer will make itself known to you when it is available.

4

Tarot 101 for Rebels

Would you consider yourself a new reader? How about a reader who is a bit dusty and needs a pick-me-up? This chapter is for you. This chapter is especially for you if traditional ways of learning tarot aren't working. Perhaps you keep returning to your deck, but it just doesn't seem to click, or you look up readings on an app but feel more confused than before.

How can a new reader find her way when there seems to be a million and one different opinions about tarot? There are also a lot of old wives' tales being perpetuated, and people pass them along without really questioning their worth or value. Just when I think that a belief has been thoroughly dead and forgotten, I see it crop up again. For some reason, bad concepts have incredible sticking power. Here are a few you might have heard:

- You shouldn't buy your own deck; it should be gifted to you.
- No one should touch your deck except for you.
- Tarot does not answer yes or no questions.
- If you charge for readings, your gifts will be taken from you.
- Reading tarot "opens the door" for ghosts/devils/etc. to use you.
- You can only learn tarot from a tarot master.
- You must use spreads.
- You must use reversals. If you don't, you're not a "real" reader.

Wow, that's a lot of rules before you even get started! If we were to follow them all, we wouldn't get any actual reading done. Let's try a different approach. First, take the pressure off yourself. Don't be quick to adopt dogmatic rules. Don't worry, you won't break anything. Tarot has been around for six hundred years; it can take whatever way you want to read it. Also, your beliefs about tarot will change over time as you evolve and grow, which is perfectly natural.

> ### Reader's Tip
> Write out a list of all the beliefs around tarot that you have picked up so far. Now, do a gut check. What doesn't feel right to you? Which ones do you struggle with? Which ones just seem silly to you? Grab a thick black marker and strike them out until you cannot read them. There, problem solved.

With that rules business out of the way, let's move on to learning tarot. The first thing I teach in my tarot 101 class is that fluency must be taught at the same time as vocabulary and technique. It should not be relegated to later lessons once you have memorized all the cards. My goal when I teach tarot is to get you, the reader, reading tarot with the first two cards you ever look at.

When we aim for fluency of reading right out of the gate, we are often quickly rewarded with sessions that will delight and surprise us, which is incredibly motivating. The other reason I think fluency is so important is because becoming comfortable with reading right away defeats anxiety, and anxiety specifically can kill our ability to listen for those intuitive hits.

I learned the value of fluency from learning Mandarin while living in China. I noticed that the way I went about learning language was different from some of my classmates. Some were consistently better than I was at acing tests; their grammar was flawless, and their writing was superb. On paper, they were better students of Chinese than I was. However, whenever we went out for lunch or to go see the sights, I was the one doing the talking. I was the one who understood a rapid-fire line of speech and translated it to the other students. I was the one who was able to speak quickly on my feet while they stumbled over their words. So, what was going on? Why was it that, while on paper they were clearly better students, I was the one capable of functionally speaking Mandarin in real life?

As they were hitting the books and studiously memorizing characters, I was in the streets. I'd be out talking to shopkeepers and sweet old ladies dancing in the park. While my friends were afraid of making mistakes, I was making tons of them. I was a great source of hilarity to the people of Xi'an. Unlike my classmates, I was learning fluency at the same time I was learning vocabulary and grammar, like children do.

Because I was learning fluency, I was able to speak Mandarin much more comfortably, even if I was not quite as technically accurate as my peers. Tarot reading is similar. Yes, you could study tarot academically and magically for the rest of your life. There is so much merit and wisdom from deep diving into the many traditions of tarot. But our focus is to read for others ASAP, and that requires fluency over textbook accuracy.

Honestly, our querents may not care to hear us wax poetic about the merits of why Strength and Justice were reversed in order in the major arcana and how that better fit a magical system. They want to know whether the cards are saying if they'll get the job. Being a querent-focused reader means not spending thirty minutes regaling them about the machinery underneath; we make it about them, and we make it accessible.

Read Like a Pro in Six Easy Steps

1. Assign only one word to each card. That's it.
2. Break your deck into piles of each type. Put the major arcana in one pile. Put the minor arcana of each suit (from Ace to 10) each in its own pile. Then put all the court cards in one pile. You should have six piles.
3. Read for others right away.
4. Read with three cards, no less than that.
5. Use a succinct question.
6. Read the cards like a graphic novel.

My goal when facilitating tarot classes is to get people reading within an hour of opening their first deck. When we work on fluency right away, we build competency as we go. This method is basically the foundation of all the other work that I will be sharing later. Let's unpack this step by step.

Step One: Assigning One-Word Meanings

Some intuitive tarot readers may not require a student to memorize any traditional meanings for the cards at all. They feel that intuition should fill in the blank. Indeed, there are many intuitive readers who read tarot without any standard meaning or tradition behind it. My feeling is this: Why take a tool out of the toolbox? Why not work to build both intuitive flexibility *and* intellectual rigor by doing both? That way, if your intuition is quiet, you can always fall back on the standard card meanings, which is what I do. I go back and forth between standard meanings and my own intuitive hits.

You don't need to learn every single possible and historic meaning of each card. Just do enough so that you can get your point across. For example, in China I would start with saying, "Where toilet?" just to get comfortable with speaking. Later I would say something as erudite as, "Would you please direct me to the nearest water closet, my good man?" Again, like children, this is how we learn language. To me, reading tarot is very much a language.

Since I first recommend only one word per card (okay, two words if you force me), it should be relatively quick to learn all seventy-eight cards. For new readers I recommend the flash card method. This was how I learned how to read Chinese. I would get a thick stack of notecards, write a Chinese character on one side, then write the *pinyin* (romanized pronunciation) and English meaning on the other. I kept them in my pocket and if I found a moment of free time in my day, I would pull them out and run through them. I found that instead of sitting down and crushing it hard on the books, I actually learned *hanzi* (Chinese characters) much more easily and faster.

Reader's Tip

On sticky notes, write one word that you think best fits each tarot card, then stick the notes on the backs of the cards. You will be using your deck as flash cards. As you go through your day, run through these instead of picking up your phone. When you feel confident that you have memorized the card, take the sticky note off the deck.

Unlike many tarot books, you are not going to find an index of tarot card meanings or even my thoughts on the matter of card meanings (outside of examples) in this book—you can find plenty of meanings in other wonderful books on the subject. There is no wrong way to choose one word for each card. Don't stress over this! We are not looking for accuracy; not yet, anyway. Go through those other books and pick a word that resonates.

Step Two: Break Your Deck

Don't attempt to tackle all seventy-eight cards at once. Start with only reading with the major arcana. Then add the minor arcana, one suit at a time. Add the court cards last. Don't feel the need to rush; the time frame is based on your comfort level. Don't bother reading reversals, just read everything upright for now. Some readers never read reversals, and that is totally okay. What's funny is that your tarot works with you to reveal the best answer or guidance—that is, its operating procedure is defined by you! Not reading reversals or doing any other tarot canon doesn't mean that your readings will be less than another's. If you do choose to read reversals later, then your readings will change to include that in the reading.

Reader's Tip

Don't worry about breaking your deck into parts, you will still get a good reading with twenty-one cards (plus however many cards you add). Tarot always seems to find a way to get its message across. If you start small and work your way up, you will be amazed to see how tarot answers questions in a variety of ways.

Step Three: Read for Others Right Away

This recommendation might be the hardest of them all. You are probably going to ignore this one (all my students do), but trust me when I tell you how powerfully quick you will gain fluency in tarot by following my third rule. Okay, are you ready? It is this: *do not read for yourself.* Read for everyone else. Read for anyone who will let you. Read for things happening in the news. Read on questions posted on advice columns on relationships. Read for people you meet on social media or at in-person tarot groups. Read about the weather. Read for your dog. I mean it—read for anyone and everything *except yourself.*

The reason for this is that when you read for others, you are not fighting your own unconscious subjectivity. Often when you are too close to a situation, you cannot accurately see what is going on. This may only frustrate you and do more harm than good. When you read for others, though, that subjective bias is usually not there, allowing your objective frame of mind to come through, instantly giving your clearer readings. So if you want a reading for yourself, trade with someone. There are plenty of tarot readers to be found in online spaces.

Reader's Tip

There are a ton of things happening in the world. Doing readings on the news can often be an easy win. Keep a journal of your readings. Then, after the situation has unfolded, go back to your journal. Were you accurate? Is there something you missed in the reading but can see in the cards now that you have context? Write all of your readings down.

Step Four: Read with Three Cards, No Less

This step might feel revolutionary—what I'm telling you to do flies in the face of just about every single piece of advice new readers get. But hear me out: stop doing card-a-day draws. When you do them, you are essentially creating a condition where you are expecting one itty bitty, tiny, little card to be able to adequately answer a question. You are inadvertently making reading so much harder on yourself. In fact, I think one-card pulls are actually more of an advanced technique.

Let me show you how that one-card-a-day reading can cause confusion.

Let's say that I shuffled my cards while asking "How will my day go?" and I pulled the Queen of Cups.

Queen of Cups

If I am learning in the standard way, I might pull out the book that came with my deck for the meaning of this Queen and see the following terms:

- Wife
- Lover
- Honest friend
- Advice
- Clairvoyance
- Understanding
- Sensitivity

Which of all of this could it mean? Is it talking about me, or someone else? Will I have a clairvoyant message? Is this who I am? Is this who I am supposed to be? All day I was on alert for my message to be revealed to me, trying to figure out what or who or how the card related to me. On the day I asked this question, I had a lot going on; I saw clients, had roofers come over to leave estimates, and finally I had to go to the ER to break a migraine.

Was the Queen of Cups me as a reader? Was the Queen of Cups the nurse who gave me the shots? Was the Queen of Cups one of my clients? I don't have any other context in the reading to help me figure that out.

On the surface, pulling one card a day seems like the logical first step, but I have seen so many students struggle with it that I no longer advocate its use for beginning readers. So, take my advice: read with three cards, no less.

Step Five: Use a Succinct Question

This step is so powerful that I dedicate a whole chapter to it later in the book. For now, when you are doing readings for others, try to get to as specific a question as possible. For example, stay away from vague, open-ended questions, such as, "How will my day go?" and turn them into specific things, e.g., "Will my boss meet with me to discuss my plans, today?" or "What does my boss think about the plan I submitted?" Use unambiguous questions whenever possible. If you are reading for someone, then work with them until you get a question that is clear-cut.

Step Six: Read the Cards Like a Graphic Novel

This is my preferred way of reading, and it's the way I will show you throughout the book. When you pull your three cards, do not assign any position (like past, present, future) to them. Just lay them out and look at them. Then, use your one-word vocabulary for each card to build a sentence.

Reader's Tip

If the sentence doesn't make sense, move the cards around. Reorder them. Make them upside down. Put them into a shape. Follow your gut on this. Keep moving them around until that little spark inside you goes, "Yes! This is it!"

Pulling It Together

Let's walk through the steps and only use the major arcana as if you were within your first hour of a tarot 101 class with me. Let's say I partnered with another student and they asked me a question.

Question: "My son has been looking for a job. Will he get one this summer?"

The question is pretty specific, so we can proceed. I pull three cards from only the major arcana. I receive: the Hierophant, Temperance, and the Hermit.

The Hierophant, Temperance, and the Hermit

My one-word meanings for these are: process, patience, and solitude

My reading: "The Hierophant indicates that your son is applying in the right ways; he is following the right process. But Temperance indicates that patience is required because it looks like he is still on his own. The Hermit for me indicates solitude. So, it does not look like he will be joining a team at a job for the summer at this time."

Let's try one more.

Question: "My cat is sick; will she get better?"

I pulled the Empress, the Magician, and Strength.

The Empress, the Magician, and Strength

My words for these are: nurturance, will, and health.

My interpretation: "With your nurturance and your cat's will to live, I see a very healthy outcome. It looks like with your good care, she will be up and running in no time."

Doesn't that feel wonderfully organic and easy? I hope so! Reading tarot should feel natural because it relies on one of the most powerful aspects of the human mind: the ability to make meaning from random pieces of information. The word for this is apophenia.

Your lovely brain will take a random spread from a deck of seventy-eight cards and make a cogent, meaningful answer from those images. You and I know, however, that the images are indeed, not random. They are very intentional in ways I think are truly astounding. I go into depth about this later in chapter 5, "If You're the Reader, Who Is the Writer?".

Reader's Tip

The goal is to find the "gist" of a reading. Close enough is good enough. If you are the kind of person who needs things to be perfect or you are looking for an exact plug-and-play system, reading cards this way may feel challenging for you. What I offer is not an exact recipe. What I offer is more like your grandmama's way of cooking: a handful of this, a pinch of that, and find your way by taste. You will find that time and practice are what makes your reading so good, not following an exact recipe.

Fluency Is the Enemy of Anxiety

Finally, I am going to jump all the way back to the beginning of this chapter and talk about the other reason why learning fluency ASAP is my go-to method: to keep anxiety from showing up and ruining a good thing. I find anxiety to be the arch enemy of a good tarot reading. When you start feeling anxious, self-conscious, unsure, or worried, all of that lovely capacity to trust and be confident in your reading goes out the window.

Anxiety is the number one killer of intuition—it destroys your ability to trust what you are reading and prevents you from reading well. I don't know about you, but when I am self-conscious or anxious, I stumble over my words, doubt what I am sensing, and basically become the thing I fear the most: a sucky reader.

Negative messages can form a feedback loop wherein we tell ourselves we might suck, so we do suck, which just reinforces the belief that we suck until we have convinced ourselves that we will never be good readers. Many readers fear this very possibility so much that they never even try to read for others; it becomes pressure rather than joy. Tarot stage fright is a real thing!

The antidote to anxiety is often confidence. In fact, when I ask my students what the number one barrier to reading for others is, the answer is confidence. What does it mean to be confident? I asked a tarot reader's group (people who are not shy about reading) what it means to be a confident reader. Here is the gist of what they said:

- Don't let doubt get the better of you.
- Don't rush, let the details speak to you.
- Trust yourself and your intuition.
- Speak confidently.
- Try reading cards in different ways if it doesn't make sense at first.
- Trust the first thing that comes to mind.
- Don't get bogged down in traditional meanings if something intuitive makes more sense.

One concept that consistently stood out in the responses was trust. For many, confidence means to trust in knowledge of the cards, to trust in your own intuition, and to trust the process of reading cards. How do we get to that place of trust? By doing a lot of readings. How do we allow ourselves to be okay with doing a lot of readings? We make fluency as much a priority as we do accuracy.

Your personal mindset is important when you read for others. It is the start of everything else we do. The clearer we are about our mindset—the foundational aspect of what we are doing and why—the sooner we get to trust, which builds confidence and virtually eliminates anxiety. Here are some questions to help you with this process:

- What do you need in order to trust what you are seeing?
- How do you trust in your relationship with your deck?
- Do you believe in your role as a reader?
- How do you show up and serve the world?
- Who are you doing this for and why?
- What is your spiritual foundation, and how does that guide your craft?
- What are the boundaries that protect you, support you, and keep you centered in all things?

Here are some things that really don't have a place within you as a reader and will actively hurt your confidence. Nothing here will be helpful—avoid these aspects at all costs:

- Comparing your journey as a reader to others. What you offer is unique.
- Locking yourself into an overly dogmatic way of reading cards. Allow for a practice that can grow and change over time.
- Giving too much credit to critics. Their opinions are just that: opinions. Make sure you are hearing the good stuff too.
- Putting too much pressure on yourself. You are a messenger. You give advice but whether people take it is not on you. You are also not responsible for knowing all things at all times. Whatever is revealed to you and how are not really up to you.

Activity
Practice the Steps

Ready to take this system on the road and see what she'll do? Great! First, review the list earlier in this chapter, in the section "Read Like a Pro in Six Easy Steps." Next, consider these sample questions. Once you are done with these, go online and find some more. The more you do, the better you will get.

★ My boyfriend is constantly raging at video games and it's starting to really affect me and I'm worried we'll get noise complaints. What is the best way forward for him to learn how to manage his temper?

★ My uncle is rebuilding his house and asked me to help. I agreed to, but lately it has been a lot of work. How do I go about asking him to start paying me?

★ I've been seeing a guy for two months and it's going well; we're exclusive and spend our weekends together. But the communication in between dates is sparse, and a part of me is feeling insecure about it. I am not sure if this is just old baggage or if this is an indication that he isn't that into me. What does his lack of communication over the work week mean?

★ My new coworker who sits next to me is trying hard to become my close friend. I'm not sure if there are ulterior motives, i.e., trying to get on my good side to get a good recommendation for her probation review. Are my coworker's friendly intentions innocent?

Extra Credit

Now go read for anyone who will let you in real time. Emailed readings don't count in my system. Remember, we have to get you using what you know in real time and on the fly.

5

If You're the Reader, Who Is the Writer?

When I started reading tarot, I thought the whole thing was pretty basic: you lay cards out in a particular pattern, and the message you get is a prediction or a piece of advice. I didn't overthink it too much. In fact, I avoided thinking about it because I thought that being "logical" would disrupt the magic in some way. I just knew that something really cool was happening when I read tarot, and I was along for the ride.

But as I started to read for myself and others, I started thinking in ways I hadn't before. What does destiny really mean? How does free will interact with fate? What is time really about, and what does it actually mean to foretell? Is the future truly knowable? Is a reading just a guess? Am I some sort of cosmic weatherman but with tarot cards? Does tarot just regurgitate my thoughts back at me? What exactly *is* a reading, anyway?

With these questions banging around in my head, I could also see that querents often had different opinions on what a reading should be. One querent's dissatisfied, "Oh well, she didn't tell me anything I didn't already know" is another querent's happy, "She confirmed everything I was thinking!" Both statements are the same, but why is one happy and not the other? Why are we not all on the same page?

What's the Difference Between Fate and Free Will?

Within each of us lies a conception about how we think the world works. This group of ideas is the lens through which we make assumptions about things and informs the way we expect the world to work. I have noticed two aspects that influence what people think a reading is: the nature of fate versus free will, and what we think time is all about.

Let me take you on a brief tour through some philosophy. There are three schools of thought that influence how people see the role of fate in their lives: predeterminism, determinism, and indeterminism. Most people have belief systems of all three in various amounts.

Predeterminism

This is the belief that some higher power is directly controlling your life, including your future. Everything has already been mapped out for you. This way of looking at the world often influences how people think of soul mates, soul contracts, and heavenly records being regularly dusted off by angel librarians.

Common questions from people who are operating from this perspective include: "When will Mr. Right come?", "Am I meant to get that house?," and, "When does Johnny get a sibling?" This belief system assumes that the future is already planned out and that we can use cards to decode what has been fated for us.

Determinism

This is basically philosophy about a determined future. Perhaps it is not as set in stone as with predeterminism, but there should be a set of outcomes from which to choose. A good analogy for this is going to a restaurant where they hand you a menu. You can choose what to eat, but you must order from the menu. There is a selection of items to consider, but you cannot go to an ice cream shop and demand lobster.

Karma is often considered a form of determinism, as is reincarnation. "I am a good person, but bad things are happening to me, therefore I must have been a miserable wretch in my past life." There is some free will in this system, but you still have to play within the rules.

Indeterminism

This is a philosophy of life that supposes things can just be…well, up to chance. Maybe there isn't a significant cosmological reason for why things have happened the way they have. Maybe it was luck; maybe things suck because of random statistical noise. In this system you have ultimate free will. You can do whatever you want and be whomever you want.

These three basic philosophies shape what your querents expect from a reading. Perhaps you are a super Interdeterminalist "I am the captain of my fate" kind of person but are reading for someone who believes God is managing every step of her way. If you read for her without laying some ground rules, there could be a mismatch.

Reader's Tip

Many readers begin a reading with a preamble or a sort of personal philosophy statement on reading or "elevator pitch" that helps manage expectations. Also, it is okay to say "no." If the querent is asking you to read on something that doesn't align with your belief system, you are not obligated to plow forward.

What Is Time?

This brings me to the other mental model readers interact with: the cultural perception of time. Our perception of time is partially innate but also learned from the society around us. How we understand time influences the way we communicate, how we build relationships, live our lives, and relate to ourselves. It also heavily influences the way we read tarot and what we think is possible as a tarot reader.

Since tarot originated in Europe, it has a traditional Western orientation toward time. The standard westerner perceives time in the same way most European languages are written: left to right, with the past to the left and the future to the right, and us in the present as the middle position. Also to the westerner, time itself is a measurable unit independent of anything else.

Think about the three-card spread of past, present, and future. Is it not a perfect model for a Western perception of time? Remember that this model for perceiving time is just a cultural agreement; it is not any more "accurate" than the way other cultures understand time.

If you came from a different cultural time perspective, you would read tarot differently. Change the culture and reading tarot could look very different.

Isn't it exciting to think about all the ways we could use tarot but don't because we are locked into our cultural way of seeing things? As a tarot reader, is it not incumbent upon us to study time perception beyond our own culturally defined one?

Cultural Differences in Time Perception

I have to tell you; I love learning about cultural differences in time perception. The more I learn, the more creatively I can use tarot for myself and others. As a reader, my work is primarily focused on the standard timeline and that is informed by my cultural background, but when I learn of a new way to understand time, I want to try it out in a reading. The results are usually pretty astounding. To help you get started, here are some of the common aspects of cultural time perception that may help shape the way you use your cards.

Time Orientation

How a culture is oriented says a lot about what is important to them. Some cultures are more past-oriented, others present-oriented, others future-oriented, and others have something extra. For example, if you were to go to West Africa, you might run into a Griot. A Griot is a singer and educator, but also the keeper of lineages. It is not uncommon for a Griot to give you the lineages of every village member going back centuries, all orally. Ask an average American about their ancestral line and maybe they could go back to a great-grandparent—until websites did the work for them!

You can also see time orientation in how a culture venerates age. Many Asian cultures have a traditional tendency toward a past-orientation, seen in how the elderly are treated as repositories of wisdom requiring tremendous care and respect. By contrast, the United States is extremely future-oriented. We see this in the way youth culture is venerated and the fact that calling someone "old" is taken as an insult.

I find it fascinating that the way we use tarot can be influenced by this orientation. A past-oriented culture might read tarot in a way that explores themes and situations that happened in the past as a way of understanding the present and future, if there is any interest in reading about the future at all. A person from a future-oriented culture may want to do a reading that is only about what's to come; they wouldn't see the value in understanding the structures of the deep past or they would consider those structures irrelevant.

Chronemics

The field of business academics has done a lot of research in chronemics because of the diversity in the way different cultures communicate time perception. These differences affect how international businesses work with one another. For example, a German saying "right away" is not at all the same as a Peruvian saying "right away." At its heart, there are two main subtypes of chronemics that would particularly interest a tarot reader: monochronic and polychronic time. These differences may certainly influence how you read tarot for yourself and others.

Monochronic time is a system in which "things are done one at a time and time is segmented into small precise units. Under this system, time is scheduled, arranged, and managed," (Cohen, 2004). Most Western cultures operate under the monochronic time system; in this system, time is usually considered a resource that must not be wasted. High value is placed on punctuality, efficiency, and time management.

Many non-Western cultures operate under polychronic time. These cultures do not necessarily see time as something to be preserved or managed. For polychronic cultures, the emphasis is on relationship over adherence to an artificial measurement.

In a nutshell, here are some differences between these cultures.

Monochronic People	Polychronic People
Do one thing at a time	Do many things at once
Concentrate on the job	Are highly distractible and subject to interruptions
Take time commitments (deadlines, schedules) seriously	Consider time commitments an objective to be achieved, if possible
Are low-context and need information	Are high-context and already have information
Are committed to the job	Are committed to people and human relationships

Monochronic People	Polychronic People
Adhere religiously to plans	Change plans often and easily
Are concerned about not disturbing others; follow rules of privacy and consideration	Are more concerned with those who are closely related (family, friends, close business associates) than with privacy
Show great respect for private property; seldom borrow or lend	Borrow and lend things often and easily
Emphasize promptness	Base promptness on the relationship
Are accustomed to short-term relationships	Have strong tendency to build lifetime relationships

These differences between monochronic and polychronic cultures change the way we read tarot, too. For example, a reading from someone with a polychronic sense of time might answer the question of "when will this happen" with a response that ties the timing to some other event, e.g., "You will get the job once your mother has recovered from her illness." If the querent in this scenario was from a monochronic culture, they might ask, "Yeah, but when, *exactly*? July? August? September? And what does my mom's illness have to do with it, anyway?"

The point here is that what you think is canon regarding how to read tarot—that is, what you consider to be the right way, what tarot is used for, how spreads should be created, or how we read cards—are all confined to your perception of reality and time. However, I think tarot is far more robust than any one perception. When we begin looking at these things from a place of curiosity rather than canon, we can become deeply creative in the kinds of readings we can do.

Reader's Tip

While the tarot deck is of course from a western European culture of origin, that does not mean it only works with that culture's framework. Go ahead and co-opt the hell out of it for your own nefarious uses. Really! Innovation comes from combining, "it's always been done that way" with "yeah, but what if we *don't* follow those rules?" The fluidity of tarot is one of the things I love most about it. The applications are astonishing to consider.

Cultural Non-Linear Time Concepts

There are also cultures who perceive time even more differently than our own. The Amondawa peoples of the Amazon, for example, do not have a countable unit of time in their language. They perceive time totally dependent upon ecological seasons or social activity. What would a tarot card reading look like if it were made by an Amondawa person?

Now I bet you are thinking, "Well, I am just reading tarot for my friends, Jenna. How is any of this relevant to me?" It is relevant to you because learning how other cultures do things gives you ideas you may not have ever thought of. For example, we rarely do readings on the "almost past" of things. We only seem to look at things that concretely happened to us but not the things that *almost* happened. Since we only see the shots we take, it actually skews our narrative of the world! But if we only adhere to the typical cultural model of time orientation, we might miss something important. We miss all the reframing we could use to become better readers just because we never considered that it could be a different way.

Let's say someone is feeling sorry for themselves. "I have the worst luck. Nothing good ever happens to me." What they don't know are the times they averted bad things, e.g., the car crash that would have happened if they hadn't spilled coffee on their shirt and therefore hadn't been running late. They will complain about the coffee drama, of course, but they won't know at all how the spill averted something far more terrible. Doing an "almost past" reading would totally dismantle that querent's concept of never being lucky. In fact, she may be far luckier than she ever realized.

Playing around with readings that do not assume a linear time system is fun! Here are some suggested readings where you can play with the notion of time a bit. You can decide how you wish to create the spread or if you create one at all.

- Instead of past life readings, do future life readings. Who are you five hundred years from now?
- Do hypothetical readings, e.g., "What would have happened if I married Timothy instead of Sara?"
- Do readings assuming that the past and future exist simultaneously with the present, e.g., "What does future me want to say to present me?"
- Do readings assuming you can change the past, e.g., "How do I use tarot to repair my timeline?"
- Do a reading for younger you as if she were sitting across from you.
- Do readings where the same cards represent both past and future.
- Do readings without time signatures and instead use relationship or casual functions such as "if this, then that."

An Absurdly Brief Introduction to Physics and Time

Reading about general and special relativity changed the way I read tarot. I pursued learning more spacetime when I noticed that my readings tended to indicate something more complex than a window into the future. The more I moved away from my cultural understanding of time as "one past, one present, and one future" toward something more nuanced, the more insightful my readings became. Specifically learning about the light cone radically changed how I view predictive readings.

The Light Cone

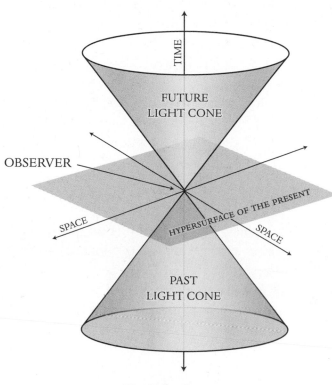

The Light Cone

Special relativity theory basically states that a light cone is the dispersal of light across time and space from a single event; the flashpoint, a singular moment in space-time. The idea is that time can only exist within the light cone as time is in relation to the speed of light. If you were a time traveler, you could only move within the cone or where the light disperses across spacetime from the event (unless you fall into a blackhole; then time would stop for you, which sounds most unpleasant).

The future is therefore not just the one and only path ahead of you. Rather, it is *all the paths* at *every single degree* radiating from you *at this very moment*. Like a tree, the future branches out before you in glorious complexity. There is no one path; it is all paths, each path made possible by the speed of light. And on each of those paths are probabilities like coordinates within the light cone in a four-dimensional universe.

So if there are multiple probabilities or futures radiating out from the event, why does a tarot reading typically only talk about one of them? It's almost as if the prediction were chosen out of the many in a subjective and skillful manner. I began to ask myself, "Why is the reading showing us this particular future out of the many? By what action is that one story told, while the rest are not? Why are we seeing one perspective? Why is the reading very focused on one small aspect rather than the big picture, or vice versa?" Asking yourself "why is this being shown to me?" is far more exciting than proclaiming, "this future being shown is the only possible future."

Reader's Tip

If the reading is talking about an aspect of the question and not the whole question itself, there is a reason for this. Ask yourself, "Why might the reading be zooming in on only this part?" It is not an accident. We are being shown *a* future, not *the* future—and there is a reason why.

How Do Paradoxes Fit In?

Now, I am going to take everything I just explained to you and throw a huge theoretical monkey wrench in the works with the concept of paradox. The nature of paradox is contradiction, and there is a paradox in particular called the causal loop. It asks the question, does a reading's prediction happen because a querent heard it and took action, and was that action the reason the prediction happened in the first place? For example, say a querent needs to get a job. The reading indicates that they will get a job in autumn for a dog walking company. After the reading, the querent doubles his efforts applying to dog walking companies in late summer, thus getting a dog walking job. Basically, the reading became a preloaded suggestion that acted as the catalyst for the prediction to come true. Here's the weird part: if the querent never had the reading, would the prediction be the same? An even stranger paradox: does a querent truly have free will knowing that their actions have been determined by a prediction, or was it fated all along? This is called Newcomb's

Paradox. As you see, the argument for fate versus free will is still a subject of hot debate.

> ### Reader's Tip
> If thinking along these kinds of lines excites you, I highly recommend delving into decision theory and game theory, following in the footsteps of the late, great Yoav ben Dov, who was both a theoretical physicist and tarot card reader. His book, *The Marseille Tarot Revealed: A Complete Guide to Symbolism, Meanings & Methods*, is on my recommended reading list.

If We Are Readers, Who Is the Writer?

If philosophy of fate determines how people read or perceive a reading and a reading is often constrained by our own notions of the nature of time, what is the reading itself all about, then? While I am not here to definitively answer that question, I can speak to what I have learned about the nature of readings based on thousands of hours of reading for others.

Something incredible emerged from the aggregate data of all those readings. In many ways, I felt there was a *presence* to a tarot reading that was not me or the querent, but rather something quite incredible. Once I was able to discern that presence, my ability to read tarot with insight leveled up big time. In fact, I can remember the first time I had an insight that clued me into another kind of paradigm, a way of reading *below* the cards.

The aha moment came about a year into reading full time. It began with a young woman who sat down for a general reading. She did not volunteer any information. I had never met her before, so I laid out my cards, excited to see what they had to say. Usually I am a diplomatic reader, but I felt an overwhelming compulsion to blurt out, "You're about to get fired!" It literally flew out of my mouth before I had a moment to process it. Both my querent and I looked at one another in shock. Very quickly, however, her shock turned into anger. The rest of the reading was trying to soften what the reading was yelling out so loudly, but my hand was forced. As the reading neared the end, I wished her a good night. While walking out the door she said, "Well my night is not going to be good, thanks to you!"

In concern, I emailed her a few days later but received no response. It was clear she was still pretty mad. She probably thought I sucked as a reader and as a person, but there was nothing I could do, so I let it go. About three weeks later, she emailed me. "Well, you were right. I just got fired. I am honestly grateful that you told me because at least on some level, I was prepared for it." After that she became a regular for years. The experience of this reading taught me that tarot knew not only what to tell someone but also how to tell it in a way that was most effective or helpful. If the message "You're about to be fired!" had been quieter, gentler, or even a little ambiguous, she would have dismissed it out of hand, possibly to her own detriment.

I realized that blurting out the message was also part of the reading. The message had to be conveyed loudly enough for her to get it. I realized that the *volume* of a reading is proportional to the querent's *resistance* to the message. Once I understood that I needed to pay attention to the content in a reading *and* how it is being conveyed, I was able to discern a whole new level of understanding.

Reader's Tip

How a reading is conveying information is just as important as the information itself. Look at the cards and ask yourself, "Why is tarot telling this person this message in this way?"

Jenna's Tarot Tenets

I was able to distill a personal philosophy of reading over the years that now serves as the backbone to the work I do, and it outlines how I have discerned that so-called writer of the reading. These tenets were written after watching what happened in the thousands of hours of readings I've had the great fortune to conduct over the years. Perhaps they speak to you, too.

Tenet One: A tarot message is one that will support the querent for their greatest good.

The message is usually written in a way that takes personality, situation, and capacity for change into account. I've never seen a reading tell someone to do something that is inherently harmful to them. Scary? Sometimes. Hard? Absolutely. But I've never seen the deck give advice that goes against the querent's best interest. I have only seen messages that were coming from a place of deeply supporting and caring for the querent. Moreover, I realized that the tarot is capable of giving the exact same answer in a million different ways. For example, if we ask, "Will Anthony come back?" the cards may say no, and they may say it in an emphatic way, a dramatic way, a soft way, or in a loving way.

How a reading decides to give information can tell us a lot about the person we are reading for. Maybe they need a wake-up call from the Universe in order to stop trying to get Anthony back. Or maybe this person is at the end of her rope, so the cards decide to take a more nuanced and gentle way of answering her question. Look at the tone. The *tone* is key to understanding where your querent really is in regard to the answer.

Reader's Tip

Sometimes a reading will not answer the question. Say someone wanted to know about their kid playing soccer, but you pull the cards and everything is about their marriage. This is what I call "tarot override," and while the phenomenon is uncommon for me, these are incredibly important. Often the tarot is trying to target what the querent is actively avoiding, or there is real danger at hand that tarot is trying to warn the person of.

Tenet Two: A tarot message is designed for action, reflection, inaction, or influence in the present state regarding a future state.

I have noticed that in most cases, the reading is not really about the future as much as it is about the querent in the present moment. In tarot, there always seems to be a DIY part of the message. Or the message about the future is written in a way to get someone to either go to that future, or avoid it. For example, let's say someone asks me when they will be in a love relationship, and the reading indicates someone coming down the road but also that the querent needs to stop playing around with her on-again-off-again ex and work on her boundaries. Most of the reading will be about what she needs to do now, with maybe a bone thrown in at the end that vaguely answers her question. The reading will be 95 percent advice from Auntie Tarot laying down that present-oriented truth and 5 percent about her future love. (Sometimes I imagine tarot as that truth-spitting aunt who loves you but isn't going to put up with your BS.)

It is not uncommon that after twenty minutes of relaying this information, the querent will ask, "Yeah, but...when is the new guy coming?" again. The fact that she mostly ignored the 95 percent of really important advice and beelined to more info on that 5 percent is a key indication that she needs to hear that 95 percent. The querent only gets enough to entice her to do the work.

If tarot gave her 95 percent advice on what she wanted to hear (the new guy) and 5 percent of what she didn't (the work she needs to do to receive that love), it would most likely cause the querent to continue avoiding the very thing that has to happen in order to meet the love of her dreams, and then the reading would be wrong. But if the reading said she would be a cat lady forever, is that really in the querent's best interest? Despite Hollywood portrayals, doom does not play a role in my readings.

Reader's Tip

Querent disappointment due to not getting what they've come for does *not* mean the reading was bad—often, it is the total opposite. Don't ask if they are happy about the reading; ask if it was helpful.

Tenet Three: A tarot message supersedes desires, wants, and agendas of the ego.

Tarot does not, by and large, care about our egos. This means that while we will get messages for our greatest good, it is not always something we want to hear. It doesn't care how much we want that job, or whether we hate our ex and want full custody. I think the number one reason reading for ourselves can be so hard is our own egos stepping in front of our perception like a mirage. We can almost see the truth but not quite.

As a reader for others, you will have to navigate the sometimes difficult bridge between the ego and the message. Many people will want a reading that satisfies their ego, something I call "fast-food" readings. How do you identify that ego-based hunger for a fast-food reading? The querent:

- Has a craving. They often just want a reading to feel better, to alleviate anxiety.
- Feels the hunger of the moment. They are not interested in long-term solutions.
- Doesn't want their problems fixed. They are only interested in final outcomes…and the outcomes better be positive!
- Doesn't want advice. They just want you to tell them the future!

Querents may pressure you to give these kinds of readings, but good luck getting tarot to play along. Usually tarot tries to sneak some wisdom in. Auntie Tarot doesn't care if you are having a hissy fit because you want pizza; she's got a nice pot of stew going, and you are going to at least try a bite! Nurturing readings can include:

- Looking at a situation holistically, not a problem in isolation.
- Knowing that resistance to the message from the querent is a feature, not a bug, and that the resistance indicates where the growth needs to happen.
- Putting the querent in the driver's seat and empowering their decisions and choices.
- Being more about the journey, less about the destination.
- Using ambiguity, nuance, and shades of grey rather than the "sure thing."

One thing I stress throughout the book is consent. You are most likely going to get sick of me talking about consent by the time you are done reading this. It is totally fine for our querent to want fast-food readings; who are we to judge them? What we cannot do is change their question on your own because we think ours is better. What we should stay away from is turning the cards to the agenda we have for them. What we can do as readers is hear their questions, see how tarot responds, and offer options. It can look something like this:

Querent: "I would like a reading on finances. Am I going to be rich?"

Reader: "We can certainly look at that. We also can look at some specific parts that are in play now that might affect that, would you like to do that, too?"

Querent: "No, I just want to know if I will be rich."

Reader: "Okay, here's the reading. It looks like you may not according to this. But the reading is also offering some advice, would you like to hear it?"

Reader's Tip

Many people come to tarot for straight predictions, but tarot rarely hands out that juicy morsel of a future without throwing in something that is required of us. Your role as a reader is to honor the session by meeting your querent where they are at, asking for consent, and offering options. Keep the querent in control of what they wish to hear.

The three tenets speak to that undefined yet benevolent sense of something greater at work within the cards. I am sure some might say, "Well Jenna, that is just you projecting yourself onto the cards." Boy, do I wish that were the case because that would mean I am fucking brilliant! As much as I wish I could take all the credit, I must concede that something beyond my pay grade is at work. Honestly, I try not to think about what "it" is as much as listen for how "it" works. I don't want to try to nail the magic down too much.

There are a few other ways I consistently see that mysterious voice in the cards that I would not call *tenets* but rather *modes of action* that are consistent. These modes of action are tricky because they can be stressful for us readers to encounter. Once I understood not just the message but how that message is crafted to evoke a response, I was able to take these in stride.

Bad Predictions to Goad into Action

I've seen tarot give a bad prediction as a way to goad someone to take action, kind of like the Ghost of Christmas Yet to Come. Remember that guy? He took Scrooge to the cemetery to show him that no one cared that he died because he was a jerk. So when Scrooge woke the next day, he changed his ways. It took Scrooge seeing his own grave to make him change; nothing but the most dramatic message would do. When this happens in a reading, it is common for the querent to see it as a doom prophecy, despite you telling them otherwise. I typically see this message occur when the querent is just not hearing that she needs to change her ways, making this the dramatic "intervention" required to get her to shift. When these kinds of readings appear, I always follow up with a statement, such as "If she makes X, Y, Z changes, does this change the prediction?" Here, using hypotheticals comes in handy. In 99.99 percent of cases, the reading changes to be quite positive.

Predictions Are Rarely Straight Shots

Just because something that said a good thing will happen appeared doesn't necessarily mean it is the *next* thing to happen. I cannot tell you how many querents have called me two months after a reading to say that the prediction was totally wrong, only to have it turn right at some point.

Reader's Tip

If someone calls you to say that something hasn't happened yet, don't panic. Encourage patience and a willingness to see what unfolds later. Also, remind them that a prediction is just that: a best guess based on what's in play and that a prediction is also influenced by the chaos of the moment. Just because you see that Mrs. Right is coming doesn't mean she will be the immediate next person you meet. And just because the reading said you would meet her through work doesn't necessarily mean she is a coworker—she could be a coworker's sister or the barista at the coffee shop next to work. Oracle work is not logical. This is why it is so powerful and also maddening.

Activity
Reverse Engineer a Reading

To help you get a sense of volume and tone, you are going to reverse engineer a reading. Below is a question and the answer. However, the answer can come through in a whole bunch of different ways.

Here are your steps:

1. Pick a spread to use for the question. Any spread will do, but use one you are comfortable with and know well. It can be an easy spread that should include at least three cards.
2. Choose one of the possible ways the answer can be conveyed using the included list.
3. Turn your deck faceup and consciously choose the cards you will use and place them where you think they should go in your spread.
4. Repeat this action for as many answers as you wish. Reflect on how different each answer looks even though they are objectively saying the same thing.

Sample Question: I just started dating Blaine a couple of weeks ago. So far, it's good. How will this go?

Answer: The new love relationship you began will be intense but short-lived.

Here is a list of possible tones/ways the answer can be conveyed:

★ Reassuring: You are going to be okay, things will get better.
★ Audacious: He was so annoying, good riddance!
★ Arousing: Get a grip, this is over!
★ Inspiring: Lessons learned from this situation
★ Admonishing: How many times do you have to do this, already?
★ Relief: It's good it'll be over soon because he isn't any good.
★ Comforting: It's over but it was exactly what you needed right now.

These are only some examples; I am sure you can come up with many more. Make sure to keep the same answer, "intense but short-lived relationship" and have fun!

Question: I just started dating Blaine a couple of weeks ago. So far, it's good, how will this go?

Answer: The new love relationship you began will be intense but short-lived.

Tone: Audacious— Good riddance!

(I am not using a specific spread; I am reading cards altogether in a straight line to answer the question. Feel free to use whatever spread you like!)

I intentionally chose:

The Lovers, Knight of Cups (reversed), Five of Wands,
Queen of Swords, Death, and the Fool

My interpretation

The Lovers represents that initial intense connection, but he turns out
to not be the romantic troubadour you thought he was. The reversal
indicates that he has turned into an inconsistent, immature, manipu-
lative man-child. With the Five of Wands, you two really start butting
heads, and once you realize this guy isn't worth your time you become
like the Queen of Swords and take your power back. You end things
quickly with the Death card, and the Fool is you leaving this situation

without any baggage or hard feelings. You do not look back and are better for it!

There is no wrong or right way to do this activity. You may see my cards and interpretation and feel they don't speak that way for you—that is totally fine! You and your deck have a language that is unique to the two of you, so choose what makes sense to you, what speaks these tones for you and trust that it is right for you!

6

Half the Work Is in the Question

Should you use a question for tarot, or should you just pull some cards out and let it flow? Does using a question somehow dilute the special sauce of a tarot reading? Or does using questions in a tarot reading help access focus and clarity? I think it all depends on your approach, i.e., what kind of reader you are, and how you want to work.

In one camp is a style of reading where the questions don't matter; the cards themselves will reveal information as needed. Some readers want absolutely no information leading into a session for fear that it might bias the reading. Many traditional spreads were built with the "no questions" technique of tarot and popular culture has accepted this style as the norm. This is a perfectly valid way of reading tarot.

Reader's Tip

To ask questions or not is absolutely no indication about how psychic or gifted a reader you are. It is simply a style difference. So, use the one that feels right to you. Over time you may find that your approach changes: going from asking questions to not at all and vice versa. It's all good! As long as you are helping people and giving them information in a way that helps then that is all that matters.

What I have noticed is that people start out wanting a general reading but usually have specific things in mind they want to see. Here is an example of a typical scenario at a party reading where the querent wanted one thing but said she wanted another:

> *Me:* "Hi, what would you like to look at today?"
>
> *Querent:* "Oh whatever, just a general reading, I don't really have anything."
>
> *Me:* "Are you sure? Anything? Because if we leave it up to the Universe, the deck will talk about anything."
>
> *Querent:* "Yeah, that's fine."

I proceeded to pull cards and realize that the reading is talking about her ill and elderly mother-in-law who needs to watch for a fall.

> *Querent:* "Really? Nothing about me?"
>
> *Me:* "Yeah, sorry. That is what the Universe wanted you to know, and time's up."
>
> *Querent:* [Unhappy grumbling noises, leaves my table and probably tells their friends about what a bad reading they got.]

Some people want to see if you can read their mind or if the subject will come up naturally on its own. Sometimes the question is not conscious, or the person is afraid to ask. Maybe they don't want to say because it is personal/vulnerable/embarrassing, etc. There are so many reasons why someone might hesitate to settle on a question, but we readers can help. There are also some other reasons why you might choose the "ask questions" route.

Reasons to Avoid a General Reading

Tarot Decides the Topic

Tarot readings will typically go toward what is most important to know at the moment, and this may not be the same as what the querent wants to know. Even when we ask questions, we can get that "tarot override" effect. That effect is magnified, however, if we go for a general reading. Some querents are legitimately okay with what comes through, but many (the majority, I would say) are not.

Preparing the Querent

Questions control the reading to a topic or category the querent is ready to hear. The direction of the reading is led by the querent—they stay in the driver's seat. With this method you probably won't run into a lot of people asking, "Will tarot tell me when I am going to die?" Questions rule out any nasty surprises that our querents are not ready for.

It Makes You, the Reader, Very Effective

Again, this is a style difference, but if you like to be concise then this is the style that might work best for you. Being a critical thinker and psychic reader are *not* mutually exclusive. You need both. The magic of tarot is robust; it can handle it!

Learning how to evaluate a narrative to find the right questions is a skill that is just as important as memorizing seventy-eight cards and a handful of spreads. Our job as a reader for others is to help our querents get to the meat; the good questions that are going to truly have a relevant impact upon their world once answered. As readers, we can help our querents find the questions within them. Here is a sample of a typical start to a reading:

Reader: "So, what brings you in today?"

Querent: "Oh, just stuff."

Reader: "Oh yeah? What kind of stuff?"

Querent: "Oh about my love life …"

Reader: "Hmm … okay, that is a topic. How about a question?"

Querent: "Well … just … how is my love life going to go?"

This vague question could mean so many things. "How is my love life going to go" could be a million other questions such as:

- I'm single and wondering if someone new is coming.
- Will Matt from five years ago contact me again?
- Can I divorce my loser spouse?

Because we still don't understand what she truly wants, we may give her some sample questions to help her narrow down a good question. A general spread could also get us here with the no-question style, but it's better to spend time looking at what she doesn't know than spending time trying to determine what she already knows and isn't mentioning. We ask her some more clarifying questions until we finally get to the heart of the situation:

> *Querent:* "Yeah, well, I have been seeing this guy on-and-off for about a year. I want to know whether I am wasting my time or not."

Ah, here is the real question that she wants answered! Why do we have to go through the song and dance of starting with a vague question when there is really a pointed question beneath it? Why do people do this? Here are a few possibilities as to why people offer vague questions or resist telling you what is actually going on:

- **Are you psychic?** If I don't tell you but you know already, that proves you are psychic (for right or wrong, this is a popular test).
- **Are you competent?** General questions are usually asked to test the waters, to see how you work and how helpful you might be. Querents start with lower effort questions before diving deeper.
- **Are you vested?** With general questions, they are looking to see if they have your full attention.
- **Are you listening?** Are you actively listening to what the querent needs, or will you jump to conclusions?

Beyond these testing-the-waters-type reasons for general questions, our querents may find it hard to identify what I call the *pain point*, the one thing in a situation from which all the other things are being affected. Often, people feel the discomfort of this pain point but are too close to the issue to identify exactly what that is, so they may craft a vague question hoping to get at what they feel but cannot quite articulate.

Let's Get to the Right Question

Funneling

Use follow-up questions to help narrow or focus the querent toward what she actually needs. One technique I use is called funneling: asking questions that begin more generally, then, as you get a sense of the picture, start asking questions that require ever more detail. In general, you start with more open-ended questions and sweep up your understanding of the situation with closed-ended questions toward the end of your process.

Example: "So, you want to know if you will be laid off? Would you like me to also ask about looking for work? Oh! You want to start a business instead? Do you want a reading on both your current work situation and also one about launching your business?"

Probing
Probing questions are helpful when you don't quite understand what the querent is getting at or you sense more detail is there that would be relevant information for the reading.

Example: "You say you are together, so are you dating, or married?"

Offering Options
Offer suggestions to add questions that allow for "what if" scenarios. As readers we can really help by guiding them to find answers when faced with making a choice.

Example: "How about we do a reading on what this house looks like should you take it, but also a reading on what it will look like for you if you don't buy the house?"

Reader's Tip
Be prepared when you ask questions. You might get pushback or sense your querent is uncomfortable. It is perfectly okay to acknowledge their discomfort if you sense it. Many people don't expect this style from a reader, so go ahead and explain why you work this way.

Are You Using the Right Spread for the Job?
A good reading consists of three pillars: a good question, a good spread (or reading style), and mastery of card meanings. Some may argue a fourth pillar is intuitive talent. Since each pillar is so incredibly important for a great reading, you will feel it if any of them are missing. This is what I call an "off reading." You can sense that it may be an off reading because it feels like you

have to fight for it or are straining to get a sense of what is going on and per-haps start overthinking the whole thing.

> ### Reader's Tip
> Once you notice this off feeling, retrace your steps: go over your narrative, make sure the question is the right one, and look at your spread. If you find yourself here, please know that it is a technique problem, not a talent problem. You are a good reader. Yes, you are! Tarot wants to be read, and it wants to be read through you!

A Vague Question with an Unsuitable Spread

Here is what a typical reading might look like if we are using a vague ques-tion and a typical spread unsuited to the purpose of the reading.

"What do I need to know about my daughter getting into college?"

Many questions start with, "What do I need to know…?" This often indicates that the situation is complicated with a lot of moving parts. But if we aren't using our questioning skills, we might soon be in hot water. A reader might choose a spread that doesn't really match the question (because we don't really know it), such as the basic three-card past, present, future spread most people get started with. Here's an example of this scenario:

We choose a basic three-card spread, hoping it will give us a general enough answer to satisfy the question. (Please note that I turn all the cards over at once to look at them. I do not typically turn over one at a time.)

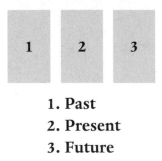

1. Past
2. Present
3. Future

We draw:
  Past: Justice
  Present: Five of Pentacles
  Future: King of Cups

Justice, Five of Pentacles, and King of Cups

So how might a typical head-scratching interpretation go?

"Okay so…hmm, Past is Justice…maybe it means that your daughter is very…err, just, she has a fair report card and her tests are good? Okay, yeah, that sounds like that makes sense, and since it sounds like it makes sense, that means it's right. Right? Present is Five of Pentacles, okay yeah it looks like you may not have a lot of money, phew, that one was easy, and future is King of Cups…hmm…that is a head-scratcher. Is the King of Cups her dad? Is this the school? What does this mean?!"

This reading doesn't feel helpful, does it? Vague question + inadequate spread = confusion. Plus, in this scenario we expected one sad, lonely tarot card to be able to speak to the breadth of her daughter's entire past experience as it could relate to college, one card for all of her present, and one for all of her future? Poor tarot! What a tall order we are asking of it! Also, why are we even looking at the past at all? It is irrelevant because the question is asking about a future state, not about something that has already happened. Further details about the situation may change the past, but we don't know that yet so we can save our reading real estate on what is being specifically asked of us.

We are wasting cards by answering questions we don't care about, yet don't have enough cards to explain what it is we really want to know. If we are only going to use three cards, we've got to be vigilant about what they are doing. By asking a vague question and using an inappropriate spread for the task, we are hamstringing what tarot can do. We are making it *much* harder than it needs to be!

Reader's Tip

Struggling is the "check engine" light in your reading. If you find yourself struggling and straining, it usually means that something is off about the question or the spread. Sometimes it means you are too close to the question, especially if you are close to your querent. However, closeness is usually not the main problem when reading for another person. If you cannot figure out what is going on, it could be that tarot just doesn't want to answer the question for whatever reason. While your querent surely wants the reading, don't do it if it doesn't feel right.

Let's try this another way and use some of the questioning techniques from earlier to build targeted questions. Let's break up "What do I need to know about my daughter going to college?" into smaller pieces. Here are some examples:

- Will she get into X college?
- Will we be able to afford her going to X college?
- Will she make a healthy adjustment to college life?
- Will her grades be good?
- Will I be okay saying goodbye to her and adjusting to my new empty-nest life?

In this case, we are not concerned about the past or present with the daughter going to college. Why not use all three cards to talk about the future, since that's what we want to know? Remember, do not only read them all as a future, read them together as a narrative. Of course, past and present situations will affect precision, but we can use our questioning skills to determine whether it will be helpful to our querent to explore them, e.g., "Is there anything in your daughter's past that you would like to know concerning this?"

With complex situations like this, I prefer to use a series of smaller spreads while asking more specific questions. This is what I call the "thin slice" technique. It is like using a small chisel to carve out little chips of marble to bring out the form of a statue. We make little cuts here and there and, in doing so, bring forth sharper accuracy.

Let's choose one of the questions above. "Will we be able to afford her going to X college?" I am choosing that one because in the first reading Five of Pentacles appeared which spoke to me as being a central issue for Mom.

"Will we be able to afford her going to X college?"

Ten of Wands, The Lovers (reversed), and The Empress

My interpretation: "Yes, you will be able to (I see the Lovers often as general intimacy as well as romance). It is going to be hard (Ten of Wands) but you are going to make it happen because you are the momma and that is just what we do (the Empress)."

Doesn't that seem so much more helpful? Doesn't it seem like it flows more easily as a reading? We don't need to keep each card in a separate little jail cell of single-card positional meanings. They like to talk to one another; they *want* to talk to one another. Later in the chapter is another example at greater length.

Reader's Tip

Do not change the question to match the cards. If your querent asked about getting a new puppy, the reading is talking about getting the new puppy. It is not necessarily talking about how she feels about getting the puppy or whether the puppy will like her. Keep the reading focused on the question. The cards are answering the question you posed, not other things. But keep in mind that this is not a hard and fast rule; there is always a "tarot override" function.

Finally, when we do a reading, we also are using readings for different things. While we all know that readings can be predictive, they can also be diagnostic (clarifying what is going on or eliminating confusion) and prescriptive (advice giving). Perhaps this is the secret fifth pillar, the *why*. Why are you here giving this person a reading? In what way are you serving them? Sometimes the answer is surprisingly complex.

Let's take a look at another example. Please note that I am using a technique that includes a third-party reading for its purposes. A third-party reading means that you are reading about someone who is not currently at your table. Some people don't do them, others do; ultimately the choice is yours on whether you will or won't.

Querent: "Tell me about my love life."
Reader: "Okay, are you single or in a relationship?"
Querent: "I am in a relationship."
Reader: "Great! Would you like to talk about a problem in the relationship, something going on with your relationship, or about where it is headed?"
Querent: "I'd like to know where it is headed."
Reader: "Hmm…okay, so tell me a little more about your relationship?"

Querent: "Joe and I have been dating for five years, but he still hasn't popped the question."

Reader: "Okay, so you want to know whether Joe will ask you to marry him?"

Querent: "Yeah, but Joe is still married. They are separated, but the divorce papers haven't been signed. I keep pestering him about it, but he still doesn't do anything. What can I do to help this along, and is this ever going to happen?"

Our querent has two needs from the reading. Since she already understands the pain point (Joe is still married) and knows where she would like to end up (married to Joe), we can create two spreads: one to clarify what is actually causing the pain point, and another to see what our querent can do about it.

- Why is Joe truly still hesitating on divorcing his wife?
- Is there anything the querent can do to help facilitate this process?

The first spread needs a diagnostic reading regarding Joe and his wife. Since we are looking for Joe's pain point, we can ask this question directly: "Why is Joe still married to his separated wife?"

Queen of Swords, Kinght of Swords (reversed), and Five of Pentacles

The Queen is looking at the Knight. The Knight is reversed, running away from the Queen and toward the Five of Pentacles.

My interpretation

Joe's wife has been possibly demanding and strict with her divorce require-ments. Her hand is out, and she wants something from him. Also, her sword is raised, and she is uncompromising. Joe is working hard to leave her (for me, the reversal here is indicating his desire to get away from his current wife.) He is off-balance and seems distraught. He wants to get away from her but feels like she still has power over him. He is worried that divorce means financial poverty.

My answer

Joe is still married because he does not have the money he needs to divorce. This is important to clarify because the reading reassures our querent that it truly is a financial problem, not that he is still emotionally connected to his wife or harbors any secret feelings about reuniting. Also, we have insight about his wife. That she shows up in the reading as Queen of Swords is very telling. (I understand that the Queen of Swords is the wife and not the girl-friend because we asked about Joe's divorce, not his other romantic relation-ship. Typically, any court cards that show up are about the people directly involved in the question.)

The wife is exerting a lot of pressure on Joe. In the reading she is looking at him, but he is galloping toward the Five of Pentacles. Also note that they are both swords cards, which emphasizes that this is not an emotional tie. That she is the Queen and he is the Knight speaks to the power differential.

There could be a lot of other things going on (kids, in-laws, etc.) but because they did not come up as the primary pain point, this means they are of less influence in the situation. In a three-card reading, usually what comes up is what is most important but not necessarily the only important things.

Now that we have reassured our querent that Joe is not still secretly in love with his wife and that this is a financial problem, we might want to change our second question based on what was uncovered from our first question. Since our querent is largely powerless over this situation (unless she wins the lottery and wants to help Joe out), we create a prescriptive ques-tion for Joe: "What is the best way Joe can quickly work on the financial problem his divorce represents?"

I don't always use three cards for every reading. Often, I keep pulling cards in a line until I get a narrative that I am satisfied with, meaning it is answering the question. The cards need to tell me a coherent story, and sometimes it takes more cards than just a few to do that. Here is what I pulled for this second question.

**Six of Swords, the Tower, Strength,
the Moon, Nine of Pentacles, Eight of Cups**

- Six of Swords: This indicates that Joe is still dealing with accepting a difficult situation.
- The Tower: Joe realizes that this divorce could turn very ugly if he does not handle it just right.
- Strength: Joe has been trying to tame the lion (his wife), but;

- Moon: The wife is not willing to work with him, she keeps him in the dark.
- Nine of Pentacles: The wife wants to live a comfortable life or feels she deserves all the money (or property) from the marriage.
- Eight of Cups: Joe might have to accept his losses and let go to be free.

Keep in mind that the question was asking what Joe should do, not what the prediction is, so every card is focused on answering just the question, "What is the best way Joe can quickly work on the financial problem his divorce represents?" Remember that each card is part of the narrative answering this question. We can also surmise that Joe might be hoping that his wife will have a change of heart and become more amicable when it comes to the financial aspect. The reading emphasizes the wife (Queen of Swords in the first reading, Nine of Pentacles in the second). She is harsh and clearly has financial motives in mind. When readings repeat information, I've learned it's because the querent needs to hear it more than once because the querent is actively resisting or in denial about the truth in some way.

While the reading is about Joe and his soon-to-be ex-wife, it is also about the querent. The tarot is giving the querent advice about Joe that will prompt her to make choices in how she wants to move forward. If I did a reading on Joe, it is likely the answer would be written in a totally different way. Remember, a reading is always taking the querent into account when revealing the message.

Keeping the querent in mind, I might say something like, "Your job as girlfriend is to help facilitate Joe's acceptance of cutting his losses to move on. You might even be able to help him alleviate his fears about financially starting over, or you two can discuss how you might rebuild your financial life together."

Can you believe that we started with "What do I need to know about my love life?" and got here? When we help a querent find the right question, use a reading that actually answers the question, and figure out what the purpose of the reading is ultimately for, we get to very powerful and helpful readings quickly.

Activity
What Are They Really Asking?
Pulling the Question out of the Story

Below are a couple of questions that represent what you might find in a typical relationship advice column. Read through the narratives and follow the questions at the end.

Example 1:
My boyfriend refuses to meet my parents.
We have been dating for three years.

I've been dating this guy for three years and you'd think we would've already made the step to meet each other's families. I will also add that we have been living long-distance for about two years, but I see him for extended periods of time about six times a year.

I haven't met his family yet. He hasn't met mine. He's normally a pretty private person. Every time I bring up the topic, he gets defensive and refuses to do so. His reasoning is that he likes to spend time with me as an escape from all the other people he has to talk to in his job. And meeting my parents is disturbing the status quo. Is this normal? I'm thinking of ending it but I'm having a really hard time. I would like to be mature about the whole situation. I have tried to talk to him, but he doesn't want to.

Example 2:
Parents afraid and sad over us kids moving out.

My sisters and I have never moved out of our parents' home. My oldest sister is thirty-two and still lives at home. We all help my parents with the mortgage and bills since my mom is getting to the point where she can't work as much. She has some savings but not enough to sustain them when she retires. My dad has some retirement saved, but again, not enough to sustain them, so he is working full time and has another job on the side. My parents immigrated from another country where it is common for unmarried children to live with their parents well into adulthood.

My siblings and I all make more than my parents, so we all have the means to move out. I am not in a hurry, but my boyfriend is. He says he hates that we don't have our own place. The problem is that I think my mom is feeling her mortality. She's realizing she's getting old and closer to death (obviously not super close but closer than she'd like). She's had a couple of her friends pass away, so she is very depressed and anxious. She is having panic attacks almost every night.

Yesterday, my sister brought up that she wants to move out, and I said I did too. My mom started crying and it made me feel so awful. I've never seen my mom cry before. I don't know how to help her or what to do. In my culture, the kids take care of the parents after the parents can't work but I want to have a little bit of freedom before I do that. What can I tell my mom so that she's no longer afraid we are abandoning her?

Questions for Each Narrative

- ★ What is each asking you to read about, specifically?
- ★ What do they need from tarot at this time?
- ★ What is the pain point? Is there more than one?
- ★ What other questions do you see besides what is being specifically asked of you?
- ★ How can you "thin slice" the questions in order to help, i.e., what was explicitly asked for in addition to the indirect questions you see?
- ★ What may not be relevant to read on at this point?
- ★ Should a reading be done from another person's perspective?

Once you have answered these questions for yourself, pull out a line of cards in a row. Start with three and only add more if you feel the three cards are not giving you the narrative. Fold in the cards and reshuffle between each question.

7

Layering Tarot Techniques

I am being completely honest with you when I tell you that this chapter was the hardest one for me to write. For the longest time, the way I read tarot was totally organic and largely unconscious. I would read for others, and when they wanted to know how I saw what I saw, I was unable to explain it. It took a long time for me to understand and then isolate all the things I was doing in a reading and why it worked as well as it did.

As you read through this chapter, you might also notice the things that you do but couldn't put a finger on. If I can help you identify what is going on with your own tarot reading style in some way, I consider that a win. If this is all new to you, then I hope I can inspire new levels of insight for you. Remember that this is just one of many ways of reading tarot, which is marvelously egalitarian that way. We all come to it from our own perspectives and it still reads faithfully, amazingly, and clearly. Yay for us!

To read tarot in layers means to build gradations of meaning in a reading. I am no baker, but when I read tarot, I imagine making a layer cake. I pass over the cards back and forth, building connections of meaning that act as a kind of scaffolding from which I then build more meaning.

Unfortunately, there is no easy rule for readings that act a little differently. However, we can identify what that feels like through trial and error by doing a lot of readings, which is why I teach fluency as soon as possible. Reading tarot builds a kind of muscle memory, you have to feel your way through, and you can only do that by practicing a lot.

You already know in some form what I am going to cover, as the previous chapters have laid much of the foundation for what comes next. So far, we've practiced how to read tarot dynamically—as a graphic novel where each card is a picture that leads into another—rather than each card in isolation in a spread. We discovered what it feels like to get psychic hits and explored the spiritual and philosophical underpinnings of what a reading is. We've also looked at how to get to the right question. These previous chapters were necessary for us to get to this part, where we pull it all together into that "layer cake" of meaning.

My layered reading technique includes two parts, twelve steps total. The first part has six steps that cover laying the foundation for a good reading, having a good question, and working through the spread to identify the narrative being told through the cards. The second part also has six steps on what to do with the narrative when you get it. In the first part, you are decoding what is being transmitted to you; in the second, you are exploring its message for meaning both in what is explicitly said as well as what might be inferred.

First we'll go through the steps to explain what I mean, then we will unpack an example together. Finally, I am going to share with you some choices you can make after the reading is complete along with plenty of extra tips along the way, so let's get to it!

Layered Tarot Reading Technique Part One

Step 1. The Reader and Querent

This is the starting point of all readings, as I believe powerful readings happen when we are relaxed and open. You begin here, from a relaxed place, reading because you want to and are comfortable with the person you are reading for. Make sure that your querent is in a receptive frame of mind. Being calm, receptive, and in a place where you two can have a reading without interruptions is ideal.

Step 2. The Question

As covered in the last chapter, you know a powerful way of working with someone to determine the "pain point" or the essential question. In my style of reading tarot, getting to the right question is an essential building block of a powerful reading. Remember that half the work of a good reading is the work of getting to the question.

Step 3. The Intuitive

After you have pulled and turned the cards upright, just look at the cards without feeling the need to immediately start unpacking the meaning logically. Remember FUMI (fast, unemotional, multiple impressions) from "Yes, You're Psychic," chapter X? You must make this the first step because our psychic hits come so quickly.

Tarot can and will trigger psychic hits that seem to come from other sources. You will get impressions and psychic hits that might not actually come from the cards themselves but are triggered by the cards in unexpected ways. Perhaps as you look at the cards you get a vivid image in your mind's eye of a room lit with shadows from candlelight. Just because it is not obviously from the cards, do not discount it. Accept everything that comes in. Blurt it all out. Don't try to speculate the meaning just yet. Just get it out, whatever you are seeing.

As you are looking at the cards, notice where your eyes are going. What are you drawn to the most? What images within the cards seem to be grabbing your attention? What might they be telling you? What feels like it flows, and what feels like blockage? What is your gut telling you?

Reader's Tip

When reading for others for the first time, tell them that there are moments where you might be silent as you are picking up on impressions. People are often uncomfortable with silence and will fill it with talking or questions, or they will just sit there getting worried. Letting them know what to expect in advance helps keep them and you relaxed. But if you aren't getting anything, just move on to the next step; don't stay here too long or take it too seriously if nothing is coming up. Sometimes we just don't get anything, and that is okay.

Step 4. The Dynamic

Look at the images. Where is there movement? If there are people, are they looking at or toward one direction, or away? What is falling or leading into one another? What about the color scheme? Is it light, dark, or does it move from light to dark? Just look at the physical properties. What do the physical properties of the imagery in the cards tell you? Even if you do not read reversals, look at the movement a reversal is indicating. Is something moving away now that, if upright, would change the reading's directionality? Is the movement being blocked in some way, or does it appear to fall off a cliff? (If all your cards remain upright, that is okay too. There is still plenty of dynamic stuff to work with.)

Reader's Tip

Your ability to read cards dynamically will vary from deck to deck. Some decks make this easier than others. If you have a deck that has less movement (for example, a Marseilles-based deck that is mostly pips), you can still use it but it may give you less information in this area. Personally, I like cards that feature people moving and doing things, as that gives me more information to draw from.

Step 5. The Categorical

How many majors versus minors are there? Are there any court cards? Are there a lot of reversals (if you read them)? Are there more higher-numbered minor arcana than lower? Does there seem to be a lot of one kind of number showing up like all sevens? Do some cards seem to be repeating themselves? If you were to categorize the cards you got, is there a pattern that you see?

Step 6. The Traditional

What are the traditional meanings for each card? If each card is a sentence, how does the group of cards create a paragraph that is meaningful? Do you find it easy to write a paragraph with these cards in a way that makes sense or, are you struggling to do so?

Layered Tarot Reading Technique Part Two

The first part of the reading is to build the story. Now, in the second part, you get to analyze the story. It is here you begin to decode the narrative to get even more information. Much of the foundation for the next steps were covered in chapter 5, "If You're the Reader, Who Is the Writer?" This is where we see that tarot sentience come into play.

Step 7. The Tone

If the reading has a tone of voice, how is it speaking to the querent? Is it yelling at them? Is it quiet and reserved? Is it gentle and comforting? What is the reading's volume? Is it shouting? Whispering?

Step 8. The Missing

Is there anything in the reading that you feel should have been there, but isn't? Do you get a sense that someone or an aspect is being withheld in some way? Look at the "white space" in the reading. What is not being said, and why do you think that might be?

Step 9. The Emphasis

We know that a tarot reading gives *a* prediction, not the "final answer" prediction. It shows us a slice of all possible paths. So, why might this particular path be shown in this way at this time? What is the reading trying to get the querent to do, understand, or reassess? Why might the querent need to hear this story in this way, right now?

Step 10. The Irrelevant

Are there any parts of the question the querent asked which are specifically not being answered? Why do you think tarot might not be forthcoming with that information?

Step 11. The Delivery

Do you get a sense that the reading is emphasizing an aspect that speaks to their unique personality trait or frame of mind? Why does the reading sound this way for this person? What can you surmise about their personality or where they are based solely on the delivery of the information at hand?

Step 12. The Follow Up

As we pass back and forth over the reading, we also find bits and pieces to add to earlier steps. You can always go back to earlier parts of the reading to add more information or nuance. This is not a static spread where once you have read it, you are done.

> ### Reader's Tip
>
> While I give you a linear step-by-step process, please don't feel the need to see it in this way. The only hard rule I have about this is to do the psychic step first. Other than that, these insights may come to you in their own unique order. While this might feel overwhelming, you will blaze through these steps in no time until it feels quite natural. In fact, you may believe all these steps are overkill, as they easily overlap one another.

Pulling It Together

Let's pull this together with an example.

Querent's Question: "I am a seventeen-year-old male. I am forever scarred by my parents' marriage. They are both strong-willed, feisty, stubborn, and at times bitter people. They constantly talk badly about each other's families. They have periods of getting along well and then periods of not getting along and then also periods of chaos, a roller-coaster marriage. It has very much soured my view on marriage, and I hate that so much. How do I get past this?"

I reformulated his story into one nice question for tarot. "What can I do to move past parental trauma so that I can be open to marriage for myself in the future?"

I pulled the Tower, Ten of Wands, the Fool (reversed), Knight of Pentacles, and King of Pentacles.

**The Tower, Ten of Wands, the Fool (reversed),
Knight of Pentacles, King of Pentacles**

The Psychic

My immediate psychic hits and insights included images of parents arguing loudly, scaring querent as a young boy. The Knight and King of Pentacles are the same person: the querent. The Tower is also the querent; he is the grounding rod for his parents' fights, and he has played a major role in his parents still being together.

The Dynamic

I find it so interesting that the Tower is in the first position, but then you see every other card being a man walking in a new direction, away from the Tower. Even the Fool reversed is walking in the same direction as the others, away from the trouble of the Tower. These images in this way suggest to me that the querent is absolutely determined not to repeat the mistakes of his parents. Note that since I am reading dynamically, I am only noticing how the reversed Fool places him in the same direction as the rest of the figures in the spread.

The Categorical

We have two major arcana: the Tower and the Fool. Numerically we have a 16 and a 0 which makes me feel like it was when he was sixteen that he began to understand how his family has affected him; the 0 is the moment where he began to break free. There are two pentacle court cards, first the Knight, and later the King, which seem to suggest his own maturation. Also, the double pentacles add a lot of earth energy to the answer.

The Traditional

The Tower (chaos and ruin), Ten of Wands (overburden), the Fool (new beginnings), Knight of Pentacles (a stable personality on a journey toward something), and the King of Pentacles (the settlement or actualization of the querent's persona) tell me a complete story: The marriage of his parents was hell for everyone involved. The querent has been and will continue the tough work toward his own evolution of being. The Fool indicates that the querent will be able to make a clean break from his past to develop as both a stable, calm, and kind young man to a fully grown one with the same qualities.

Reader's Tip

I do not cover reversals too much in this book, but if you find you are struggling with the reversal in the example, let me tell you what I do. I read reversals if they appear to add to the narrative, make sense of it, or deepen it in some way. If it feels like the reversed card is a stumbling block or just does not flow with the other cards, read it as upright. It's okay. The tarot mafia are not going to come for you, and your readings will not suffer.

The Tone

I feel like the tone here is reassuring and centered on the querent. I get the sense that the reading is saying, "Hey, you don't have to worry about this. You will never be like them, so your marriage could never be like theirs." The tone acknowledges his fear and really allays it by reminding him of who he is, his essential nature.

The Missing

There are a couple of things missing here that are interesting to me. The reading decided not to reassure the querent by giving him a prediction about him being married. It did not really answer, "How do I get past this?" The reading is not actually answering his question directly, but rather is reassuring him that he will be fine.

Fascinatingly, the reading appears to answer a deeper question the querent asked subtly. Let's look at his question again, focusing on these subtle points. "I am a seventeen-year-old male. I am forever scarred by my parents' marriage. They are both **strong-willed, feisty, stubborn,** and at times **bitter** people. They **constantly talk badly** about each other's families. They have periods of getting along well and then periods of not getting along and then also periods of chaos, a roller-coaster marriage. It has very much soured my view on marriage, and I hate that so much. How do I get past this?"

If you are listening closely, you will see that our querent started off talking about his parents' personality traits. While he didn't say it outright, my feeling is that he believes the marriage is not working because of their undesirable personality traits. What I think he is really asking (and the tarot is absolutely answering) is, "Am I doomed to become like them?"

What is also missing is bad news. There is nothing to indicate that he will fail in love and marriage or that he is doomed to live a lonely, broken life in a cave somewhere. *The absence of a good prediction does not mean a bad prediction.* Communicating that the bad prediction is also missing is important because we do not want our querent to jump to conclusions that are not necessarily true.

Reader's Tip

Even though I used up a whole chapter to help you get to the right question, it can still trip you up as it did for me in this example. What is astonishing is that tarot knew anyway and answered the question so deep in the querent's heart that neither one of us saw it for what it was at first. In fact, I could only see his real question by looking at tarot's answer and determining why it was answering the question in the way that it did.

The Emphasis

By indicating who he will become (Knight to King of Pentacles), the reading is emphasizing that the querent is and will remain a stable, thoughtful, generous, and ultimately drama-avoiding fellow. On a meta-level, I hear the reading saying that it is personalities and how people deal with conflict—not marriage itself—that makes for a good or bad marriage. I understand that this key concept must be stated explicitly to the querent. My intuition tells me he needs to hear this specifically.

The Irrelevant

The reading basically dismisses the querent's "how do I...?" request, which indicates to me that while he feels that his parents have soured him on marriage, this is not actually the case. With that Fool to Knight to King of

Pentacles run, I feel that once he has moved out of the house and into his own life, his feelings will change around this matter. He feels as he does now because he is in the thick of it, but the reading emphasizes him moving on so fully that I have to state it explicitly. "While you are worried about this influencing your future married life, I think it may not feel as impactful once you move out."

The Delivery

Our querent is still trying to figure out who he is and also needs reassurance that who he is becoming is someone quite unlike his parents. My sense here is that it is possible he is who he is because of the role he played as the lightning rod (Tower); he took their fire and found a place to ground it.

The Follow Up

After working through this reading, a few more additional insights came to me. The reading is predictive about what will happen and who he will become, so I believe that the parents are on their way to divorcing, and the querent doesn't know it yet. The Ten of Wands also indicates both his role in moving past them and also possibly in helping his parents as they end their dysfunctional union.

While I tried my best to pull apart the different aspects of a reading into steps, as you can see, there can often be overlap between them. And you may come to conclusions wherein you cannot quite explain how you know what you know. That is your beautiful intuitive mind chiming in. With time and practice, it should feel pretty fluid and natural.

Reader's Tip

Some steps will not be clear to you, and that is fine. If you feel like you get stuck on a step, don't sweat it. Just skip it and keep going. It may hit you later on in the reading or not at all. It will still be a good reading. Some things tarot decides to play close to its chest. Part of being a good reader is knowing when the information is not available and just working with what you have.

You can pull out a lot of juicy information with a few cards if you look at them through different lenses. While this seems like a lot of steps, it will happen naturally with practice and time. Your ability to glean so much information from a few cards will delight and astound the people you are reading for.

Activity
Identifying the Layers in a Reading

Below is a question I have supplied plus the cards that I pulled for it. Your activity is to fill in the steps.

Sample Question

"Whenever anything happens, my mom's first thought is that someone is trying to sabotage our family or our things. For example, a hole ended up in our tent and she claimed that our spiteful neighbors had come over in the night and done it. There's a lot of examples of her exhibiting this type of thinking.

"Growing up, I always took everything she said as fact. As I've gotten older, I am feeling like the issue isn't the people around us but more her interpretation of a situation. So, whenever she says something potentially paranoid, how can I ground her thinking without gaslighting her? She becomes really stressed out because she feels like the whole world is attacking her, and I just want to help out. In short, how do I help my mom reframe her paranoid thoughts and do it in a way that is not dismissive of her?"

Seven of Pentacles, Six of Swords, Nine of Pentacles, Nine of Wands, and Queen of Swords

Part One

- ★ The Intuitive: Initial psychic impressions
- ★ The Dynamic: How are they moving?
- ★ The Categorical: How many majors, minors, numbers, etc.?
- ★ The Traditional: Traditional meanings pulled together into a narrative

Part Two

* The Tone: How is the reading speaking? And why?
* The Missing: What feels like it should be there but isn't?
* The Emphasis: What is the reading spending its time talking about, especially?
* The Irrelevant: What does the tarot seem to be actively ignoring?
* The Delivery: Why is this particular story being told in this way?
* The Follow-up: Anything else you are getting as you work through the reading?

8
Court Cards Are People, Too

Whether the question is about job interviews, marriage troubles, exasperating teenaged children, or why that coworker down the hall is such a jerk, most querents want to know about other people, themselves and the relationships between them. By and large, if you are reading for someone, the reading covers one of these topics:

- Understanding a situation or person
- Advice concerning a situation or person
- Getting a prediction about a situation that involves people
- Understanding how they are being seen or understood by others
- Learning about who they are or are becoming

To read tarot for others is to read about people. Which cards in the deck represent people? Court cards! So when you nail the court cards, you will absolutely kill it when reading for others. Over time, court cards have become my favorite cards in the deck because they can do so much.

Many readers struggle with getting the feel of court cards. They are often the last cards new readers understand well because court cards don't just represent people; they can also represent actions, advice, or states of being in a reading. These possibilities make them the most flexible (and maddingly complex) cards to work with. To add to that complexity, the court cards have a long history of correspondences and attributes that may cause more confusion than clarity.

Beware the Correspondence Tables

Some of us looking for that "plug and play" system of reading might find relief in correspondence tables to give us a clue as to whom a court card may be.

For example, the Queen of Cups has often been corresponded with beauty, pale skin, light brown hair, hazel eyes, the astrological sign of Cancer, and a wife. But if we are looking at a court card as an equation that never changes, we might miss what tarot is actually telling us.

When I started reading tarot for myself, the Queen of Wands would always show up to indicate that the reading was talking about me. However, if I had followed the traditional correspondences for Queen of Wands, I might have dismissed what my own deck was trying to tell me. The Queen of Wands traditionally corresponds to a fire sign in Western astrology, but my sun sign is not a fire sign. If I was just going off of tarot correspondences alone, I might have missed a powerful insight about myself.

The Test of Time

Over the years, the court cards have been added to and built up with every subsequent generation of deck creators and authors. These meanings act as an imprint from a time where it was more relevant then but may not be so now. You can see the history of these meanings easily with a word cloud. Dump all of your books that came with your decks, tarot books, and online resource court card attributes into a word cloud generator. The more times a word is repeated, the larger it gets. The largest words are often the oldest. Here is one I did for the Queen of Swords.

Queen of Swords Word Cloud

What is fascinating (if not unsurprising) is the Queen is assigned words that are stereotypical to traditional women's roles. You see several words indicating widowhood (spoiler alert, "widower" appears nowhere in any King in the deck I found) as well as her inability to have children. A woman was once defined by her role as wife and mother. This word cloud clearly illustrates that legacy.

While I believe it is worthy, necessary, and helpful to read on tarot history to get a sense of how things have been done in the past, the lens of culture shifts. So how do we decide what to keep? We get to decide that for ourselves, but an informed approach is a great jumping-off point.

Let's take a brief tour through three different books to show you what I mean. Below are the descriptions of the Queen of Wands from Waite's *The Pictorial Key to the Tarot* (1910), Gray's *A Complete Guide to the Tarot* (1970), and Cynova's *Kitchen Table Tarot* (2018). I've **bolded** words and concepts that are the same between the three while *italicizing* things that have changed over time.

Waite: The Wands throughout this suit are always in leaf, as it is *a suit of life* and animation. Emotionally and otherwise, the queen's personality corresponds to that of the King, but more **magnetic**. Divinatory Meanings: A *dark woman, countrywoman*, **friendly**, *chaste*, **loving**, *honourable*…also, a **love of money**, or a certain **success in business**. Reversed: *Good*, **economical**, **obliging**, *serviceable*. Signifies also—but in certain positions and in the neighborhood of other cards tending in such directions—**opposition**, *jealousy*, even *deceit* and **infidelity**.

Gray: Choose this card for a *blonde with blue or hazel eyes*. Divinatory Meanings: She has great power to **attract that which she wants**, and is **fruitful in mind and body**. **Loving Nature** and her home, she is **practiced with money and sound in her business judgements**. Reversed: **Domineering**, **obstinate**, *revengeful*; likely **to turn suddenly against another without cause**. If married she could be **unfaithful**.

Cynova: The Queen of Wands is *funny* and **warm**. **Grounded** and *calm*. She's **friendly** and **welcoming**… She has lots of **energy**, lots of **confidence**…. Divinatory Meanings: Wands are about *fire and action*…the black cat is a sign of her *edginess…strong and independent…grace*…. Reversed: It's about being truly *self-serving. Selfish, bitchy*, and with a **nasty temper**….

Her confidence either pulls inward to *shyness* or lashes out in *aggression*. This woman is *fierce*.

Let's compare themes of commonalities. Some language use has shifted over time, so I am using more modern descriptions. What themes has the Queen of Wands held to over time?

- The capacity to attract things or people to her
- Welcoming
- Energetic
- Confident
- Friendly
- Loving
- Good with money
- Good at business
- Practical
- Creative
- Helpful to others
- Controlling
- Difficult on purpose
- A cheater

A lot has remained true about the Queen of Wands. These foundational aspects of the Queen are aspects that you can rely on when describing the court cards realistically. And yet, some things have also shifted over time.

What has shifted:

- Physical description to none at all
- Wands shifted from representing a social class to representing an element
- Sense of humor

What has been added over the years:

- Fierce
- Aggressive
- Strong
- Independent-minded

Our Queen has a bit of a rebrand going on! Traditionally, each suit corresponded to a station in society. The swords were nobility, the cups were clergy, the pentacles were the merchant class, and the wands suit was understood as the suit of peasants and servicepeople. You see this in Waite's description of Queen of Wands as he uses the words "countrywoman" (and "dark woman" as in tanned from being in the fields) and "serviceable." The card itself, however, gives a greater nod to the Golden Dawn's wands-to-fire element correspondence. It would seem here that Waite was trying to marry the older understanding of this Queen with his magical system. He melded the two, and over time the fire association took hold until many readers today are unaware of the older country girl association.

In fact, it would appear that the Queen of Wands of a hundred years ago tracks more closely to the Queen of Pentacles today. All of this matters because you see that the Queen of Wands rebrand was to make her "fierier" and feistier of temperament. Our new Queen is also strong and independent-minded; she isn't going to serve anyone, no ma'am!

See what I mean? There isn't really any "canon," but there are layers, and as some layers are applied others are washed away.

Knitting Together What Works for You

Basically, each court card is a modern-day Frankenstein's monster. Your job as a reader for others is to decide which collection of parts works for you. Here are some guidelines to help you with that process:

1. Pull court card descriptions from three to five sources spanning a large time frame.
2. Determine if there is anything you would like to add—everyone puts their own spin on it.
3. Decide what feels relevant and helpful to your querents. Keep the helpful, dump the rest.
4. Now make them real.

> ## Reader's Tip
> Meanings shift and change over time. Focus less on making the court cards the most accurate and more on making them human. The more real they are for you, the better you will be able to convey who they are to your querents.

Breathe Life into Each One

This next part was inspired by an old book that I find myself returning to every now and again. I highly recommend it (or one like it) for work such as making the character of each court card come alive. It is called *Your Mythic Journey: Finding Meaning in Your Life Through Writing and Storytelling*. Using their format as a jumping-off point, I am going to give you a list of questions to help you build each court card into a personality so real they will sit on your shoulder and whisper into your ear during readings.

The Public Self

This is the part of the court card that is easily discernible by others.

- What is the first thing that people notice about this court card?
- How does this court card walk?
- If they had an hour off for lunch to do whatever they pleased, how would they spend it?
- What do they want to be known for?
- The office gossip wants to tell you something about this court card; what might it be?

The Private Self

This is the part of the court card that few see.

- If this court card could break one law without penalty, what would it be?
- What is this court card envious about?

- What does this court card fear other people finding out about them?
- What does this court card daydream about?
- Which other court card does this court card secretly wish to be?

The Unknown Self
This is a part of the court card that lies unconscious.

- What recurring nightmares does the court card have?
- What did the court cards' parents fear the most?
- What triggers this court card, and what does that look like?
- What might this court card avoid looking at?
- What role in the family does this court card play?

Once you have a fairly decent write-up of a court card, you can then distill what you know about them into narratives your querents can easily absorb. Think of them as your own personal scripts that give you a foundation as you work with querents.

Here is a write-up I did for the King of Pentacles based on his mythic journey and if he were a love interest I wanted to tell my querent about.

King of Pentacles in Love
The King of Pentacles is a sucker for tradition. He is the kind of guy who will court you with dinner at the nicest places and tickets to whatever you fancy. He isn't the most creative King in the pack, so do not count on this guy to surprise you—you have to communicate and let him know what you want. If you like physical affection, this is your guy. He cannot keep his hands off of you! He is always seeking out your hand or touching your leg; physical touch is a major love language for him.

The King of Pentacles plays for keeps. This King is the kind of guy who will almost never ask for a divorce; only the most egregious transgressions would make him leave once he has committed. Keep in mind, though, that he is a little old-fashioned. On the plus side, this means that he will move mountains to provide and protect. Want to be a stay-at-home spouse? He couldn't be happier. For independent partners, he might come across as too confining. "If it ain't broke, why fix it?" is a motto he believes in.

Interacting with the King of Pentacles

Write a script explaining who this court card is as if they were your querent's lover, best friend, sibling, boss, child, or parent. Once you have done that, change what you say depending on which court card you have picked to signify your querent.

Would I say the same thing about the King of Pentacles to a Queen of Cups as I would to a Queen of Swords? Not necessarily. I might emphasize some things about the King that are particularly relevant or challenging about each Queen. The Queen of Swords may need to know that this King likes his creature comforts while she is out protesting in the streets. The Queen of Cups might need to know that this King has a love language that is more about fixing something broken in the house than writing poetry.

★ ★ ★

These parts of reading for querents are not necessarily "readings" in the traditional sense. The reading reveals the cards, but your knowledge of how these court cards interact with each other provides a depth of revelation that can be extraordinarily helpful. Being able to look at a reading about an interview and deeply describe the boss and what they are looking for is invaluable to the job seeker, for example.

The next few pages feature some tips and tricks for seeing court cards in surprising ways. These techniques are ones I rely heavily on in sessions, and they tend to ring true over time. The court cards are always so surprisingly malleable; just when I think I have learned all I need to know about court cards, they surprise me once again.

Use Gendered Decks in New Ways

A friend of mine who was assigned female at birth consistently pulled the King of Wands. We would joke about that "Big Daddy" energy, but it all made sense once he transitioned. There was another friend who was leaving her heteronormative marriage and kept asking about love only to have two Queens appear. When I asked if she had romantic interest in women, she blushed and gave me a shy smile.

Many decks are moving away from gendered expressions of their suits and court cards, but keep in mind that a traditional deck does not necessarily always result in a traditional reading or meaning. Don't judge a book by its cover! Tarot is timeless in this way, so let it surprise you.

Reader's Tip

Play it loose with gender. Do not discard what initially appears as a mismatched gender—it may be indicating something you do not know. However, if it doesn't feel right to read the card in a gendered way, move inward by describing personality instead.

Court Cards as Age Versus Maturity

In the same way that gender can be more of a suggestion than a rule, so it goes for ages, I typically do read Pages as children, Knights as late teens to early thirties, and Queens and Kings as adults. But this is, shall we say, a bit loosey-goosey. When it is not a direct stand-in for approximate ages, I also tend to see court cards as expressed maturity level and power within relationship dynamics.

There have been more than a few times that someone's full-grown boyfriend appeared as a Page. It is also not unusual to hear that said grown adult man is living with his momma. I've also seen grown adults appear as Pages when the reading is about something that delights them. There is something about the subject matter that brings out an innocent joy in them, or they are starting something completely new.

I've also seen elderly parents with dementia or any other illness where they have to be cared after like children appear as Pages. One of the saddest expressions I have seen, however, is a grown parent showing up as a Page while their child, a minor, appeared as a King or Queen. My philosophy when it comes to tarot is this: *rules usually work until they don't.* And when they don't, there is a big reason why, so keep up!

Reader's Tip

Keep to the personality types as your key to help you from getting confused when you see role reversals.

Hints from the Hierarchy

If a grown adult is looking to settle down and showing up as a King or Queen but their partner is a Knight, watch out! That Knight may not be ready to put roots down yet. By contrast, healthy couples tend to show up as the same type in their relationship dynamics: Page to Page, and so on. But if one person is a Page and the other is a King, it might indicate a power differential or, more traditionally, an age difference.

Suits Point Toward Interpersonal Dynamics

If we assume that the suits are stand-ins for elements, they can tell us a lot when we are looking for compatibility between two people. Two people with the same court card elements may indicate an ease with one another while a fire and water persona together may be more dynamic. Think about how earth and water might get along, or fire and air. Do they feed one another or smother the energy? Do they slow down what is rushed, or do they extinguish it altogether?

For example, let's say that a Queen of Cups is in a relationship with a Knight of Wands. First, there is the hierarchical aspect. The Queen to Knight indicates a power or maturity imbalance. Second, water extinguishes fire and too much fire turns water into steam. This indicates to me that the Knight of Wands may find the Queen of Cups too stifling and fear her putting a wet blanket on all of his fun. The Queen of Cups gets energized by that fire energy, but too much and she literally burns out. Pro tip: don't try to domesticate a Knight of Wands, but you can go along for the ride!

Cherish Each Court Card as If They Were Your Own (Because They Are)

As you get to know the personalities, be careful to watch your own biases. Every court card has an equal mix of good and unsavory character traits. So if you find yourself focusing too much on the negative traits and not letting the court card's character show up in positive ways, (or vice versa) you have a bias you need to resolve. We will cover this further in chapter 12, "Judgement Is a Card, Not a Reading Style."

When it comes to learning the court cards, more is more. Read all the booklets that came with your decks, tarot books, and online resources to get a full sense of all the possibilities that can play into each card. You don't have to do this in one sitting; your understanding of each court card personality will grow alongside your tarot journey. With some research, time, and practice, each court card will begin to feel like they are sitting right next to you. Make them come alive.

Activity
Tarot Tinder—What Happens When They Swipe Right?

Take your court cards, shuffle them, and pull two at random. Now imagine that they have just made a match on a dating app and have both come to see you for a reading about their relationship. Explain to them what their strengths are together, how they best communicate, and potential problems to watch out for. Offer your advice as if each court card were sitting across the table from you.

King of Pentacles x Queen of Swords

Strengths

Both can be ambitious, and both want to be seen as important to others. This Queen will make sure that no one takes advantage of this King. In fact, she will work hard to protect their legacy and wealth. This King can rest assured that he has a fiscally responsible partner.

His calm demeanor doesn't challenge her, and she feels like she can be herself around him. His quieter nature and easygoing manner comfort her. She is witty, smart, and loyal—all pluses in this King's book. This Queen dislikes drama, does not manipulate others, and is clear about her needs; all of this is received well by this King.

Communication Style

Swords is verbal and likes to point out things to fix which can grate on this King if she is too blunt in her (usually correct) observations. This Queen is fast; her thoughts are a mile a minute, but she needs to give this King time to process. If she pushes him, she might find that his mouth opens, but nothing comes out. This Queen will be rewarded if she can cultivate more patience because he needs time to gather his thoughts and words. If this Queen needs a conversation partner, she would do well to find one among her friends because this King is typically a man of few words. When he does speak, however, it is careful, measured, and wise.

Challenges

The essential issue is that this King usually subscribes to traditional gender roles. He has an idea of the kind of woman he wants in his life, but this strong, ambitious, intelligent, and independent Queen doesn't have time for that silliness. She wants him to accept her as she is, while he wishes for more nurturance from her. She shows affection with loyalty and would fight for him to the ends of the earth, but this King may not recognize that as affection and may feel unattended-to as a result. When this Queen is angry, she grows cold and distant, which is hard for this King to work with. He feels punished and pushed out by her. As a result, he will become avoidant, which makes her angrier, creating a toxic cycle they can get stuck in if they are not careful. To break the cycle, the Queen needs to learn to be more vulnerable, and the King needs to learn to confront.

9

This Is Why Court Cards Are Hard

Now that you have a strong foundation of the court cards as people, I am going to share with you my techniques for understanding whether the court cards are talking about a person, an action, or a psychological state as well as some general guidelines for how court cards tend to act in readings, at least for me. I also include examples that illustrate the properties I am sharing with you while also building on how to read tarot from a layered and intuitive perspective. This chapter is a bit technical, so if you are totally new, you can skip ahead now and return later when you are ready.

It's in the Question

How do I know whether a court card is talking about a person, an action, or an inner psychological state? By the question, of course! This technique is once again based on chapter 6, "Half the Work Is in the Question." When we get to a tight, well-structured question, we are able to assign the court cards to the role they will play in the reading.

I've built my own internal court card "rule book" based on thousands of hours of readings for others over the years. As with everything I share, I am not trying to give you an equation that works the same way every time like a mathematical equation. Rather, I am giving you possibilities that may help your own practice when reading for others. Over time, you will get a sense of what works for you. As always, your intuition trumps any guideline I can set before you. Always trust yourself first.

Tips for Reading Court Cards as People

1. **If the question is about the querent**, typically the first court card out is the querent or an aspect of the querent in regard to the question.

2. **If the reading is about someone else**, I will often read the first court card as the person the querent wants to know about, not the querent, unless it is clear that the querent is the first card by type or personality.

3. **If a question is about both the querent and others**, then the first card is usually talking about the querent, subsequent cards after that are also people. But, this is not a hard rule, I go by innate personality characteristics to decide who is who. Sometimes I will ask the querent, "Who does this remind you of?" and give them a description so they are telling me what court card is them versus another.

4. **Sometimes court cards show up to indicate people yet unknown.** Because querents like to immediately identify a court card as someone they might know, communicate to them that the card may be someone not yet in their lives, unless you sense it is.

5. **If a querent asks about a love relationship but only one court card appears**, it is often an indicator that the relationship is distant, or the tarot wants to make the reading concentrate on the querent's personal journey rather than the relationship dynamic. Refer to chapter 5, "Layering Tarot Techniques," where we look at "what is missing."

6. **Personalities first, then action states**. This means that I tend to read court cards first as people involved in the situation, then as actions if all the people are identified.

Let's do an example of a reading seeing court cards as people. Just like the other readings I have shared, we will begin with a straightforward question and pull three cards while reading them in a line altogether.

"I want to buy this house, so what do I need to know about the sellers in order to win the bid?"

The Knight of Cups, the Emperor, and the King of Cups

First, notice that the question is the sellers, not the house. Many readers would focus on the house outcome and skip over that the question is really about the seller.

Since the question was about multiple people, I am reading the court cards about both of the sellers. And since the question was asking about the sellers, I do not read the court cards to also include the buyer.

What I see

The Knight of Cups is looking at the Emperor while the King of Cups is looking away from the other two. The Emperor is sitting impartially between these two court cards. For me, this indicates that the King of Cups is over it, and he wants to sell and move on. The Knight of Cups, however, is in the weaker position (here I am using the hierarchical nature of the court cards to assist me) but it is the King calling the shots. My intuition is telling me that the Emperor is the house. The Emperor is solid, on his throne, and corresponds to the number 4. These are all things that, for me, speak to "physical home."

Both parties are swayed by emotions as both are represented by the more emotionally centered Cups suit. Looking at the two Cups cards may also indicate that the selling of the house has to do with a separation or divorce. They are both in their feelings, and not on the same page.

In this reading, the sellers are represented by the Cups suit, indicating individuals coming from an emotional place regarding the sale. However, this does not necessarily mean that the sellers are Cups people all the time. Keep in mind that tarot is showing us information relevant to the question and the querent's best interests, not the objective unalienable truth about the sellers.

Tips for Reading Court Cards as Action

What do we do if the question is looking for advice or action but the court cards show up? If the court cards are not people, then what do they represent? Here are some of my guidelines for court cards when they indicate action:

- *Pages:* Messages or new beginnings in things that that suit conveys
- *Knights:* Searching for, moving toward, or moving away from what the suit conveys
- *Queens:* Being cared for, or caring for others in a way that the suit conveys
- *Kings:* Arrival, completion, or achievement in the way that the suit conveys

Court card reversals means things that are not communicated, haven't begun, aren't moving, are not cared for, and have not been achieved.

Let's do an example of what the court cards look like from a place of action and or advice.

Question: "What kind of offer should I make to win the house?"

Here is what I pulled.

The Moon, Page of Swords, and King of Swords

What immediately comes to mind is that the court card progression (Page to King) is the key to answering the question. Because I did not ask about people, I do not read these courts as people. I am reading both the Page and King as the offer itself.

My interpretation of the reading
Obviously, this is a situation with a lot of unknowns with the Moon in the first position. The situation feels unclear or perhaps things keep changing. The offer itself is represented by the Page of Swords. Moon to Page of Swords could mean that the offer should be made while things are still unclear. It's as if the lack of clarity within the situation somehow gives the offer an upper hand. It can also mean that the offer is a total shot in the dark. Page of Swords indicates that the offer made is honest. But the last card being the King of Swords means that whatever the Page represents is too small of an offering. The offer needs to "grow up" to be bigger, more solid, and more transparent on the details as the King of Swords can often represent clarity and truth. Once the offer is made, however, stand firm. The King of Swords makes a decision and does not waver.

> ### Reader's Tip
> Be careful not to take wide detours by deciding the court cards are something else. The cards are answering the question. Stick to it!

Tips for Reading Court Cards as Psychological States of the Querent

My favorite way of reading court cards are as internal, psychological aspects of the querent. I love reading in this way as it helps the querent explore themselves and their own personal growth. This is what I think tarot really does best. Plus, I usually get interesting questions around this topic and not the usual laundry list of day-to-day life worries.

1. **More than one court card** can indicate the person's evolution or growth (or backward devolution) in the reading.

2. **Court cards can indicate different facets of one person**, their process through a situation, or personal development. In these cases, I often see more than one court card as expressing different schemas or aspects of the person, e.g., the triggered self versus the relaxed self, the inner child versus the adult, the person at work versus the person at home, the spiritual self versus the mundane self, and so on. Seeing court cards as personality traits or even as traumas can be really helpful in unpacking internal challenges or revealing patterns or habits the querent would like to change. For example, in love-based questions it is not uncommon for me to see the querent have two Queens: the inner vulnerable Queen of Cups being guarded by a Queen of Swords. We talk about how we might be able to integrate these two aspects a little more fully.

3. **Court card reversals** as people often indicate where the negative traits of that court card are being expressed loudly. I get the sense of someone in a less healthy version of themselves.

4. **Knights reversed can mean a triggered person**. With the four triggered states being fight, flight, freeze, and fawn, we can see how Knights reversed in psychological readings indicate trauma being triggered in some way. Knight of Wands = flight, Knight of Cups = fawn, Knight of Swords = fight, and Knight of Pentacles = freeze.

5. **Adults who consistently show up as Pages** often indicate inner child work, or areas of childhood pain that is being provoked by a situation.

6. **People shift as court cards**. We all have our "native" court card—the person we normally are—but court cards can appear as advice, such as "You need to take on this type of personality or outlook."

Let's do an example from the place of seeing the court cards as internal aspects.

Question: "I never really saw myself as a homeowner, and I fear that I will become boring (i.e., like my dad). Will home ownership turn me into someone I don't really want to be?"

Here is what I pulled:

The Fool Reversed, Knight of Cups Reversed, and Page of Pentacles

The Fool reversed speaks to a fear of growing up. The Knight of Cups reversed and looking right at the reversed Fool tells me that the querent may feel as though they have not finished their adventuring years or found the right person to settle down with. But the Page of Pentacles in the final position is wonderful here because the reading reassures the querent that they are still young with plenty of flexibility and curiosity. The querent is reassured that they get to be both things: open to new experiences but also settled to a certain extent.

The Knight of Cups reversed tells me that the life they are living is not actually fulfilling. They chased after a lot of dreams, but for various reasons, those did not pan out. Also, Knight reversed is often a trauma reaction for me (fawning.) So, I wonder if he is just saying yes to please his dad while keeping his reservations to himself.

The Page of Pentacles tells me that the querent will enjoy home ownership and take good care of the home, even if he might be younger than his peers when he buys one. The querent will like taking care of the house and enjoy hosting people there. He will surprise himself by how much he actually likes it.

A question about home ownership is often about physical items and wealth. The Page of Pentacles suggests that the querent is well on his way toward building that foundation. His rambling days might be over, but from the firm earth beneath them, they can build more amazing things than they ever could as the reversed Knight of Cups.

Because this reading emphasizes a fear of growing up, the Page as the last card is a lovely message that definitively reassures the querent that he won't sacrifice that open, flexible, and supple quality—only add to it.

It is not an accident that I have devoted two whole chapters to court cards. As a reader for others, court cards tend to have an outsized role in readings. They truly provide their proverbial weight in gold when answering the querent's questions.

If you can nail court cards in readings, you can confidently read just about any question placed before you. As a tarot practitioner, I encourage you to continue to study and deepen your understanding and skill with the court cards. Even after more than thirty years of study, they still surprise me and truly light up my readings in ways that no other cards can.

Activity
Person, Action, or Personality Quiz

What follows is a list of questions that can help you determine whether the question is one that needs a courts-as-people answer, an action answer, or a psychological state answer.

Go ahead and answer them! If you don't get any court cards from your initial three-card draw, keep shuffling and pulling until you get at least one.

★ *Question:* My half-siblings don't think of me as a real brother. I try hard to make them care but it doesn't work. How can I get them to love me like a full sibling?

★ *Question:* My girlfriend got dressed up in a revealing outfit to go to a festival with friends. I don't want to be a controlling boyfriend but I feel insecure and jealous. How can I work on this?

★ *Question:* I have a final interview for what I would consider to be my dream job. But I don't know much about the people I will be interviewing with. Is there any way I could find out what they are like?

★ *Question:* I'll be working my second consecutive summer camp and winter weekend camp this year, and I was recently offered a Sunday morning position to work alongside my head coach that might result in me being an official coach by the fall. However, my parents don't want me to accept it because "we've always gone to church as a family," and they're refusing to help me get there. How can I convince them to help me take advantage of this opportunity?

★ *Question:* I have a blind date coming up this weekend. Other than some pics and a few texts, I have no idea what I am getting myself into. Can you tell me more about her?

★ *Question:* My girlfriend gets irritated when she is short on cash and her financial stress impacts our relationship. She has two kids but doesn't get child support for either of them and refuses to go after the fathers for it. I feel really uncomfortable with the quality of life the kids have had as a result, and I am upset for my girlfriend but she won't do anything. I don't know what to do. Should I push her to do more to help her situation or just let it go despite my discomfort?

★ *Question:* My bio father whom I haven't spoken to in five years and rarely saw through childhood has decided he wants to be my father again, and I can't fathom what that would even look like. What would an adult child/parent relationship look like between us if I decide to build one with him?

10
Being the Reader They Need

Over the years I've been the recipient of many readings. I have had my face read in China, my coffee grounds read in Turkey, I also had a South Korean shaman toss for my fates with divine objects. I've had readings done while sitting on a cardboard box and readings done while seated in a luxurious villa. If a reading is to be had, I want in on it. Many readings I've had were fantastic, and some were atrocious. Sometimes that difference had to do with the skill of the reader with their craft. A bad reading is a bad reading, no way you can fix that. But I have also had amazingly good readings that came from bad facilitators. What I mean by that is that the reader was very good at reading with their tool of choice, but everything else surrounding the session was terrible. I've gone to readers whose reading rooms reeked of cigarette smoke with ash all over the furniture and tables, not to mention peeling skin flakes everywhere. Sure, the reading was pretty good but how could I relax when I was afraid to touch anything?

One reader made his own cartomancy system using comic book imagery. It was so fascinating and cool! But his wife was listening down the hall and stomped down the hall very loudly past us into the kitchen to clearly indicate that the reading was over—I got out of there quickly.

I've had readings from friends who were distracted and others who were having a bad day. I've had readings from people who spent the whole time reading about something I didn't care about while glossing over the most important thing. These experiences made an impression on me as I began to read for others.

As a result of my experience, I thought about not just the reading itself but what I as a reader could do to make the entire session as querent-oriented as possible. In what ways can I be the reader they need? How can I facilitate our time together to ensure that my querent feels comfortable, heard, and cared about? Those things are just as important as a good reading, whether we are reading for our bestie or someone paying us for our time.

I've also made plenty of mistakes along the way. There have been times where I have failed my querents, where I was not as attentive or present as I should have been. Some things I only learned as I went along. We all make mistakes, and that gives us the opportunity to do better the next time.

Below is a list of things I think are important to consider. There shouldn't be a distinction between the reading and the session that the reading is contained in. The more receptive querents are to the reading because they are comfortable, the easier it is for you to read for them. It's that simple!

Preparing Yourself

There is no right or wrong way to prepare for your reading, but there is one hard rule: put your personal issues away. Burn incense, meditate, and stuff them in the closet with the rest of the skeletons. Whatever you need to do, do it. Along with your personal issues, how you feel about your querent should be set aside too. They deserve your positive (or at least neutral) regard. If you are annoyed by them or dislike them, you cannot give them the reading they deserve. Be honest with yourself—if you secretly dislike your sister-in-law, do not read for her. You are not the reader for her.

Space

Setting the stage is important. Do you or your querent have access to a space conducive for a reading without interruption? Can you lay your cards out on a clean, flat surface without a toddler's sticky little hand grabbing hold? Attention is respect. If you give your time and attention, then your querent must offer the same.

Reader's Tip

Now that video readings are such a thing, the number of querents who log in with their phone propped up on their dashboard while driving or who are out jogging with the phone while it shakes up and down giving you vertigo is more common than you would think! Make it clear to them about the kind of space they need on their end so that you can conduct a session with them.

Audience

Now, readers can differ in what they like, but will you allow others to listen in on the session? Is it okay if they bring their friend, or partner? What about the kids? Personally, I only allow another person if I am doing a reading specifically about their dynamic, as in a relationship reading. Other than that, I allow no one else in the session. I dislike audience members for a few reasons. My clairvoyance will often pick up their stuff instead of the querent's, causing confusion. Also, the querent won't be as honest or vulnerable with me when someone else is in the room. Group readings in a party setting is fine, but for private work I want it to be just the two of us.

Reader's Tip

If you are reading for people online using, say, an online video platform, make it exceptionally clear that they must be alone in the room with you if you don't want an audience. I cannot tell you how many times querents had people just off-screen that they "forgot" to mention were there. I don't know about you, but I don't like someone listening in on the sly. Consent has to work both ways.

Keep Small Talk to a Minimum

When acting as a reader for a querent, even a friend, decline to talk about yourself too much until the session has ended. How you talk about yourself or what is going on in your life may inadvertently influence the reading. Plus, it is asking the querent to provide emotional labor for you which places them in the role of service, not you. This is fine to do once the session is over, but at the start make it about them. Reading time is special. Make it sacred.

Recording

Will you allow your querents to record sessions? I allow recordings because I think they help the querent replay and listen for what they didn't catch the first time. We are always listening through the lens of the moment, but readings are often bigger than that. Things we didn't pay attention to in a reading can become the most important thing, but we won't realize it until later.

Recording also helps keep what was said straight. Querents will come back saying you said things you know for a fact you did not say. Their subjective memory will put words in your mouth but with a recording you stick to the facts.

If you do allow recordings, do not ever forget that your querent may not be the only person who will listen to it. Keep in mind that the guy she is complaining about may be the next one who listens in. This happens quite often because the aggrieved party (usually the person seeing you) wants to use the reading as a data point for what might be wrong in the relationship. It is used as a, "See? She doesn't even know you and she said such and such, therefore you need to listen to her." If I sense that the relationship is especially fraught, I will mention to my querent that the reading is particular to her and what she needs to hear. I add that if her partner were to come in, they might get a totally different reading. I also refuse to read for individuals within a relationship if it is toxic, as that is a conflict of interest for me. If the partner comes my way wanting to straighten things out, I refuse to have that conversation. Even if my querent decided to share her recording, I hold to confidentiality no matter what.

Note-Taking

Some readers do not take notes, but I do. I forget just about everything that happens in a session. After the session, I write no more than a paragraph somewhere safe in a place only I can access. I include the situation, first names of people involved, and a brief overview of the reading. This is helpful because if they come back for a reading you review your notes. I've had querents come back after three years and talk to me like I should remember every detail! The more readings you do, the easier it is to start confusing them, so writing it down helps. Make sure, however, that you keep these notes somewhere only accessible by you. A password protected place is best.

Choose a Deck Wisely

I remember buying one deck with glee only to find that the only fat body in the whole deck was the devil, accentuated with empty plates laid around her…talk about problematic! Even if I personally did not find that triggering (believe me, I did) how could I possibly in a million years use a deck like this knowing full well that some of my querents have larger bodies?

Querents feel more comfortable if the deck reflects them, and diversity should be standard in your deck choices. The Modern Witch Tarot is a lovely synthesis of diversity. Fully melanated decks such as Dust II Onyx and decks that depict people with disabilities such as the Next World Tarot are also suggestions.

Reader's Tip
Consider your audience when reading with strongly thematic or political decks. You can always have "your" deck but use a public deck or even a variety of decks depending on whom you are reading for. While I may love my super pagan witchy decks, they aren't for everyone. I choose for the querents or, better yet, give the querent a choice of decks.

Shuffling

Do you shuffle or do you allow your clients to? Do you cut the cards and have them pick piles to read from, or do you take from the top? Do you fan them out and let them pick each one? There are many ways that you can do this and I find each one works just as well as the other.

The only caveat I have is that if the querent is in a highly emotional or anxious place, I will pull the cards for them. I have noticed that high emotions or fear from the querent means they infuse the deck with those emotions, very likely causing the reading to reflect what it is that they fear. So I do it, acting as a buffer so we can see the cards neutrally.

Introduction

I've mentioned this before, but it bears repeating. An introduction from you at the start of the reading is helpful because it tells the querent what to expect from you and the session. Here is where you want to lay out the logistics, expectations, and boundaries. Ask the querent if they have questions for you, and then begin!

Pregnant Pauses

Sometimes you need a moment. Perhaps you are getting multiple impressions, or the cards are particularly challenging to pull together. Your querent may not understand that you need a moment and so they often will fill in the silence with extra questions. If you are one who needs a moment, make sure to tell your querent at the start of the reading.

Reading Choreography

Basically, I see sessions with querents as a dance. There are steps to this dance that when I am faithful to them, allow a reading to go beautifully most of the time. We want to think about the session as a whole in addition to individual readings within it. What I share below assumes that you are doing readings for a friend casually, or with a querent where you have some time to spend with them.

I typically ask my querents for their questions at the start of the reading. I want to see the "laundry list" of their needs and from there I can determine the best way to approach them with the time we have. I also ask them what is a must-read from their list. I want to make sure that I hit the most important thing and give it the most time.

> ### Reader's Tip
> Some querents will talk a lot about one issue because it is top of mind, but that doesn't necessarily mean that that topic is the one that they want the most time on. Make sure to ask what their order of importance is so that you can plan accordingly.

Usually I start off with a lighter question from the list, which allows both of us time to relate to one another and get comfortable. Then I will go for the meatiest question, the one that caused the querent to seek out the reading in the first place. This is where I will most likely spend the bulk of my time. Depending on how long that takes, I will close with another lighter question, or a question focused on something empowering or fun.

If your session is just one question, I still recommend thinking about having a beginning, middle, and end. Perhaps the beginning can be something as simple as a one-card pull that speaks to the energy around the querent, followed by the question, and finally another closing card pull like a final message.

Querents often ask me, "How many questions can one hour cover?" And honestly, it's all over the map. Sometimes one question is so huge that even one hour will not do it justice while other times we can do up to ten; it depends on the querent and the complexity of their situation. I cannot possibly know that until we start diving in.

Do General Readings Last

You already know how I feel about general readings, but if you must do them, move them to the end of the session. When a querent tells me that they want a general reading, I explain the process and that if they have a specific burning issue, I would prefer to look at that in depth, first. Once that is done, we can move to a general reading.

I have a variety of general readings I can do depending on the time I have left. At its simplest, I have a very simple four-card spread that takes me anywhere from five to ten minutes. From there, I can do a fifteen-minute general reading all the way up to a thirty-minute general reading. The difference between them is variation in topics and, of course, detail. This allows me the ability to give them a general reading depending on how much time we have left after we do specific reads, and these general readings will typically catch anything that has fallen through. But even when we put all of these measures in place, we may not be able to make everyone happy all the time, which brings me to the next topic.

Reader's Tip

Move the general reading from the first thing you do to the last. When you do it this way, you can spend time on the burning issue at hand, then choose a general reading of your choice as a "sweeping up" function that catches whatever you did not hit on until then.

Interpreting the Reading Faithfully

There seems to be an idea floating around that asking an oracle a question assures that we will get the answer we want at the level of detail we want and that the answer fits all of our questions in a logically consistent manner. Boy, wouldn't that just be great?

Tarot is not an analog version of Google; it is not going to answer a question to the letter without leaving anything out. The Universe makes us work for it, even when it gives us hints. That is just how speaking to the Divine is. But if the reading is too vague for the querent's liking, they may prompt you with questions and push you for more detail than the reading is giving. This kind of pressure may cause you to speculate (take a rational guess at something) or add more detail than is really there. Interpreting faithfully means speaking the reading and *only* the reading. We are all entitled to ask the Universe anything we want, but we are not entitled to dictate how the Universe answers it.

Reader's Tip

You are not a bad reader because you cannot tell a querent the exact day they are getting a job. You are not a bad reader because your querent is demanding excruciatingly precise details that you are not seeing in the reading. Don't force an interpretation to make a querent happy. You are the messenger; you are not the one writing the message.

Check-In

Check-ins are a way to invite the querents to add their own perspective, nuance, or insight. When they interact in the session (and don't merely sit back and watch as if you are on display as a road show psychic,) they buy into the process. It is about making sure that a querent is hearing the message as you intend. By "checking in" I mean asking pointed and directed questions, such as "How did you feel about that Eight of Cups coming up in that way?" or "What are your takeaways from this reading?" Stay away from vague questions like "So what do you think?" because the answer may be just as vague.

Check-ins when we invite querents to add their own perspective, nuance, or insight are best practice. When querents feel they are part of the session, and not watching like you are on display as a road show psychic, they buy into the process. Because they are part of building the reading, they take it to heart.

Reader's Tip

Querents going extra still or quiet usually means they disagree with what is being said. Often, those disagreements come from the way you worded the message. Also, it could be that they heard it in a way you did not intend. Let the querent explain where the disagreement lies. If you think it is a communication snag, reword the message to see if that helps it click.

Callback

The callback is a technique I learned from watching stand-up comedians. In it, they end a show with a callback: a joke hearkening or linking to something said at the beginning of the show. The technique is employed intentionally to create a sense of group bonding. It makes the audience feel good about the experience/show and the comedian. It also has the effect of closing a set wonderfully.

I use callbacks in two different ways; first as a way of thematically linking readings happening later in the session to earlier ones. As I notice lessons being repeated or insights that look different but are really the same, I draw it to the querent's attention. I also use a callback as I close the session. I will mention a particularly salient point that came up again and I might even do a final oracle card pull on it. Energetically, this works to nicely close the session. It also shows the querent that we are listening, paying attention, and remembering what was said to them. It signals that they are important to us.

Don't Be Afraid to End Sessions

Sometimes you may find yourself having to end a reading because you cannot be the reader they want you to be. Perhaps they want you to do mediumship and you aren't a medium, or you were asked to do something that goes against your ethics. Whatever the case may be, if a querent is trying to get you to do something or be someone you are not comfortable with, do not push yourself to make them happy. End the session. Yes, it will be awkward. Yes, it will be hard. End the session.

One time, a querent came to me who had recently lost her mother. She started to have dreams of her mom who was trying to tell her something, so the querent started to see mediums and channelers to figure out what the message was. The querent was told by others that her mother's dream was a series of instructions for opening a shelter for trafficked exotic animals. Apparently, her mother was indicating that there was a treasure buried somewhere and if the querent could get to the buried treasure before the feds (who knew about this treasure but didn't want it to be revealed) the querent could then use that treasure to help the animals.

The querent came to me wanting me to literally mark X on the spot for the treasure! At the start of our session, she shared maps with me of places other readers had told her to dig. Every time she dug, nothing was there (surprise, surprise). She mentioned how she was running out of money and needed to find this treasure before she went broke. I could not continue the reading. Everything within me was screaming at me to end the session ASAP. I ended it, and she was angry and disappointed. She tried to push me to continue the reading and told me how disappointed she was. "Couldn't you just try,'" she asked. I said no many times and basically had to push her out the door. Ending sessions is difficult because querents want you to give them what they came for, even if you tell them you cannot.

Oddly—and this has never happened before or since—right after I ended the session, I instantly ran to the bathroom and threw up. I was ill for two days after that; it felt as if I had been exposed to a great darkness and my body reacted violently to release it. The reading I was asked to do was not only dangerous to the querent but also energetically poisonous to me.

Reader's Tip

Listen to your body when you are conducting readings. Does a querent give you a headache whenever you read for them? Do you feel tired, drained, or sad? Do you find yourself getting ill after being in the presence of that person? These are not random occurrences—something is happening on an energetic level between you and the querent that is toxic to you. Chapter 16, "Ready for the Woo?" investigates this topic in more detail.

Remember, you retain the right to end a reading at any time, for any reason. If you feel uncomfortable, you know you cannot help them, or if they have a problem that you are not equipped to handle, end it. If you feel unsafe on any level, end it. Please don't even feel obligated to continue no matter how the querent is acting. Ending the reading is a mark of strength. Knowing when you are not the reader they need is just as important as everything else.

Closing

A session needs to be gradually wound down before it actually ends. It is a good idea to signal to your querent that you are headed toward the end a good ten to fifteen minutes beforehand. You need to state explicitly to your querent the time left and what is possible to do in that time. Don't just spring the ending on them.

The wind down is the reason I tackle the meatiest question in the middle of the session and also why I ask for a list of questions at the start. The last thing I want to have is a querent sobbing over a difficult reading with five minutes remaining and I have to leave; it's irresponsible for a reader to do.

We want to build the whole session as best we can with the beginning (ground rules and discovery), the middle (the main theme, lesson, or information), and the end (the wind down, bringing back to center, grounding, and returning to the ordinary).

The wind down is not the time for one more quick question. In the past, I would try to offer one more simple question trying to give them as many readings as possible, but that often backfires. I have learned the hard way that many querents don't understand what a "simple, quick question" means for a tarot reading. Even if you tell them what you can do, they will most likely tell you the next thing they want to know regardless of complexity. It is okay if you cannot get to everything. Strive to be a reader who gives quality over quantity.

Besides doing another reading, you can consider another activity during the wind down such as pulling an oracle card as a final message, a mini grounding meditation, or prayer or intention. These are all nice things to do that are quick, help bring you both out of the reading vibe, and act as a lid to the session. Sometimes I even chime my meditation bell to signal the end.

Activity
Journey to the Oracle

Seek out at least five readings from other readers (hint, hint). These can be from people you know, or you can buy one from a professional. Honestly, I think it is best to get a wide variety of readings. Perhaps one from a casual friend, one at a festival venue, one from one of those walk-in places, one from someone you admire, and if you can afford it, one from someone who charges on the higher end. After each reading, run the experience through the guidelines shared with you in this chapter. Ask yourself what you liked about the experience and what you did not and why. What did the reader do well in addition to the reading, and what may have needed more work? Next, compare and contrast each reader. How were they alike or different from one another? What did one do well that another did not? Where do you see yourself in relation to these other readers? Your comparison is not about judging readers to see who is the best—rather, it helps you know what it is like to be on the querent side of the table from a variety of readers. These insights will only make you more mindful about your own practice.

11

Beyond Predictions

Ask anyone on the street what tarot is for and they will say, "to tell the future." That's valid. You can certainly use tarot to predict things. But tarot is no one-trick pony. Tarot is more like a Swiss army knife; it has a variety of functions. But there is often a disconnect between what the average person thinks tarot can do and what we know tarot is capable of.

We readers certainly have our work cut out for us. We have a lot of educating to do, especially if we are the type of readers who don't use predictions in our readings. So, let me ask you, what would you tell someone who asked you what tarot is for? Can you readily list off all of the wonderful things tarot can do? Where have you seen tarot help and how do you communicate that clearly to querents?

I have a few ideas. Below is a laundry list of things I think tarot is really good at doing outside of the prediction aspect. These are not going to include tarot technique (except for the activity at the end). These are topics as jumping-off points wherein you get to decide how to showcase these aspects in your own unique way.

Clarifying Relationships

Most querents use tarot to understand romantic relationships, but tarot is good for exploring all kinds of relationship dynamics: parents, children, siblings, friends, and bosses. We can explore others beyond predictions by asking questions such as: "Why is she like that?" or "How do I help make this better?" or "How do I accept that this is just the way he is?" In my experience, I've noticed that much of our choices hinge on whether someone else will change. If they don't, do we accept what is, or do we make changes for ourselves? Tarot is a tool like no other for rapidly and clearly showing us what we might otherwise avoid. But it can also show us what is going right by belaying our fears and showing us when something is working even better than we dared hope.

Reader's Tip

Querents may ask questions that they may not be ready for. Some querents will tell you that they want a reading that is "all truth and no chaser," but when you proceed, they are devastated. If you sense that a reading may be moving into territory like this, give your querent options that are more exploratory and less final.

Rewriting Painful Narratives

Tarot is great at telling stories. Each of us operates the way we do because of the stories we tell ourselves. Some of those stories are incomplete or incorrect. With tarot, we can rewrite those stories within us; when we do so, we unlock tremendous healing. For example, let's say that a querent had a breakup with someone and is ready to do a reading about the next relationship, but you can tell that the last break up was recent. The querent is still upset, and closure did not happen, or closure happened in a way that was traumatic. Of course, the last thing your querent wants to do is spend time going over that failed relationship, but what if what they think about the relationship (say, that their ex told them that they were too needy, which is why it ended) isn't actually the case? As the reading lays out the real reason (the ex was afraid of commitment), we can help the querent find peace.

Showing the Outcome of Inaction

Change is hard. We can ruin our lives holding onto something because the fear of the unknown is greater. A reading can clearly illustrate what a life can look like if the decision to remain the same is made. The sunk costs fallacy can keep someone prisoned to something that is making them miserable. Showing a querent clearly, the cost of inaction can help goad someone into making those changes that are needed.

Reader's Tip

I often find that a querent is drawn to get a reading from some nonconscious aspect of themselves. Call this our higher selves, our unconscious minds, or our guides. It is as if they are being dragged to the reading to hear, loud and clear, the thing they have been avoiding. They need to hear the message that is already inside of them spoken out loud to make it real. This is also one of the reasons why you might have a querent coming for the same question over and over again. Sometimes, it just takes five times before they are able to act.

Giving Permission

So many of my readings with querents are really about voicing the permission they are struggling with giving themselves. Many querents—hell, all humans, I mean, come on—struggle with trusting our gut and our decisions. A good reading can grant permission: to leave a relationship that is not working, to leave the job that is abusive, to go no-contact with a family member, to become the person they know is inside them begging to be let out, to take the trip, to get the tummy tuck.

Offering Hope and Inspiration

Often, querents will want a reading when things are dark in their lives. They wonder if the sun will ever rise again, and they come to a reading hoping to hear that message. This is totally different from "make everything magically okay," which some querents *do* indeed wish for—who wouldn't? It's best to use tarot to inspire querents by reminding them of who they are and what they are capable of. We can use tarot to show querents that in most cases, things do get better, provided the querent is also doing the work. I think many people are afraid of putting in effort that may come to nothing. Readings that help them see how their efforts can positively affect their lives in practical ways are terrific motivators.

Replacing Anxiety with Control

Personally, one of the most interesting and helpful ways I use tarot with querents replaces anxiety about things they cannot control with actions they definitely can. For example, if someone asks, "Will my book become a bestseller?" This is a loaded gun of a question, and questions like this usually arise from a place of anxiety. Consider "Will I ever get married? Will I ever be happy?" These blanket questions assume only two options: relief in the yes, or terror in the "no. But neither the question nor its answer assumes that the querent has a say in how it goes and why. These questions do not allow space for free will. What we can do instead is build a reading pointing to what is within our own ability to control. We can ask questions, such as "What habits am I maintaining that may sabotage my success?"

Helping Process Grief

Many querents will come for a reading because they are grappling with grief. This may be literal grief of losing a loved one, or some other loss like losing a relationship, or job. One of the hallmarks of grief is asking yourself the same questions over and over again, looking for greater meaning in the suffering.

Grieving people are often looking for the "why." Why did that guy come into my life just to wreck it? Why was I shown this dream job and then fired? Using tarot to answer these questions eases suffering and helps the aggrieved find peace. It can help them understand how their suffering has meaning. Whether it was to learn a lesson, or because this choice leads to other ones along the way, or we need a witness to hold space for our pain—tarot can do all of these things.

Reader's Tip

Read more books. Read books on philosophy and psychology. Read books on theology and human nature. Read books on pain and resilience and growth. Reading books about the human condition gives you a greater vocabulary when relaying tarot's message. The wisdom in others' pages will inspire your own and add depth to your readings. Less social media, more books. You'll find book recommendations at the end of this one.

Illustrating Destructive Habits While Advising Healthier Ones

Tarot is excellent at showing querents how their choices directly feed into the life they are living. Using imagery, we are able to help querents see what they couldn't before. In the same vein, tarot can also offer healthy replacement habits and help a querent see that changes they make will in fact change their lives for the better.

Opening Spiritual Pathways

Some querents come to a reading because they feel the spiritual call to do so. People may ask questions such as what repeating patterns or numbers mean, e.g., why do they see the number eleven all the time, or why they always dream of cardinals. One of my favorite questions someone asked me in a reading was, "How can I best please my god, Loki?" The answer was as fabulous and funny as you can imagine.

First and foremost, we can use tarot to act as a bridge, a revealer, and witness to our own spiritual unfolding. We can use tarot to read on past life or future life work. We can do readings that focus on other worlds connected to us interdimensionally. We can do a reading asking a specific deity to step in and speak. We can ask the Universe what we need at this time, how to know we are on the right path, and if that strange dream we had the other night has deeper meaning. To divine means to speak to the Divine.

> **Reader's Tip**
> Querents tend to seek a reading when they are having what I call a "teething" moment. Like a teething baby, querents can feel the discomfort of something about to emerge, but they usually have no idea what it might be. Often they will describe it as a spiritual feeling with increased dreams and synchronicities. This moment before the breakthrough is a powerful time to have a reading.

Encouraging Acceptance and Accountability

Querents will often come to a reading when they feel they are out of options, when all of the easy answers have been attempted, or they feel so stuck they cannot see a new way through. Tarot readings for querents at these crossroads often give a few answers that usually take two paths: one, an approach to try that you have not yet considered, and two, the approach you need to take is one that you do not want to. What is *not* going to work is doing the same thing hoping for a miracle.

For example, I had a querent who took a series of exams for his work but it was found out that for some reason, the certification was never recorded. He had a new job offer that was contingent on the certifications. He wanted to fight the certification board to instate what was their mistake. The reading was clear; he would have to retake the exams. Of course, this was the last thing he wanted to hear, and the reading turned difficult as he processed his resistance to an unfair situation. Only a small part of the reading was about what was actually the case. The rest of it was helping him to accept what was unavoidable and to lean in to retaking the tests. There was also a component that was predictive. In his case, it showed him acing the tests without much effort. He ended up passing the tests in time to start his new job. Without the reading to help him make the best of a bad situation, he may have continued to fight the certification board at the cost of the job. And just maybe hearing that he would easily pass the test changed the outcome. Could this be the causal loop paradox? Perhaps!

In so many ways, a tarot reading is not "just" a tarot reading. It is not uncommon for querents to say something like, "I did not realize how much a tarot reading could be like therapy." This is because they have not been previously exposed to the incredible skill tarot has at lifting veils, revealing truths, and bearing witness to their lives. This style of reading tarot is not for everyone. Some querents do not want this kind of reading at all and that is perfectly fine as long as we let them know and give them options. Some readers only want to use tarot in non-predictive ways and that is perfectly fine if we are communicating our approach and giving the querent options.

But for me, my best work lies in both places. I want to facilitate healing *and* tell the future. If I were to refuse to "fortune-tell" then perhaps I am lending too much weight to a hard answer where there doesn't really need to be one at all.

Activity
WOOP (Wish, Outcome, Obstacle, Plan) Spread

Sometimes querents are so focused on the final outcome that they downright ignore all the good advice you gave them to make that outcome happen. They might call you six months or a year later to tell you that your prediction did not come through while also conveniently forgetting their role in making that prediction happen. There is a disconnect between what you said and what they heard. Somewhere in the course of the reading, they ignored or outright rejected the "if" part that led to the "then" scenario. However, we can make spreads that emphasize personal responsibility toward the outcome they desire as well as the mental restructuring model to help them see their part in building good outcomes while neurologically reinforcing what is revealed in the reading.

The WOOP spread makes some changes in how we read tarot by putting both the wish and the desired outcome first, while emphasizing the behavior and plans that the querent needs in order to even make that outcome a possibility. A system developed by Gabriele

Oettingen, author of *Rethinking Positive Thinking*, WOOP (Wish, Outcome, Obstacle, Plan) is based on twenty years' worth of scientific data on how to get people out of the trap of wishful thinking and also teaching them how to get out of their own way. For our purposes, we are adding tarot dynamically, which can drive the message home even more powerfully. Here is what the spread looks like.

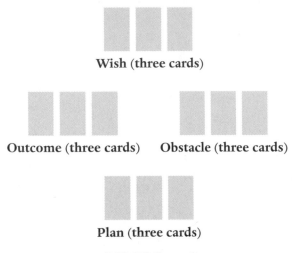

Wish (three cards)

Outcome (three cards)   **Obstacle (three cards)**

Plan (three cards)

WOOP Spread

Pull three cards for each station. You can decide whether you want to use reversals. At the first two stations, choose each card specifically, faceup. For the second two stations, put your deck facedown, shuffle, and draw as you normally do.

Wish: Turn your deck faceup. From there, consciously select three cards that best illustrate your wish. A wish is a positive thought, goal, or outcome about the future.

Outcome: Keeping your deck faceup, once again consciously choose three cards that look like the best possible outcome of your wish. Once you have them out, sit with them and really imagine the cards coming to life in your mind's eye with the outcome you desire. If you are using this spread with a querent, don't worry if the cards they choose are not "technically correct"—we are just going for how they connect to the imagery and what it means for them. Additionally, invite your querent to explain their card choices. Why did they choose that image? What does it mean to them?

Leave your cards out; do not reshuffle them back into the deck. With your deck facedown once again, shuffle and draw from the deck as normal. When using this spread with a querent, the second two parts are the parts you will conduct with them as a reader while they listen.

Obstacle: What is within you that holds you back from fulfilling your wish? What is your main inner obstacle?

Plan: What is needed? What behavior or habit changes do you need to overcome the inner obstacle?

Now read the cards as a narrative. "My wish is (x). When I plan to (y), then the outcome of (z) becomes possible. What follows is an example of the WOOP spread in action with a querent.

Wish

Querent's Wish: I wish I could accept myself just as I am.

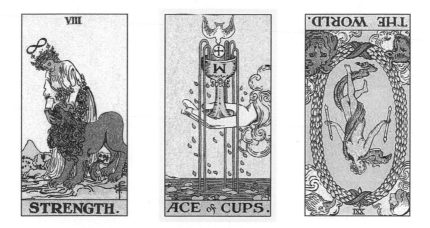

Strength, Ace of Cups, the World (reversed)

Reader: "Tell me about these cards that you chose. How do they illustrate your wish?"

Querent: "With Strength I see myself being in a place of wholeness, where every aspect of myself is working with the other without friction. The Ace of Cups reminds me to love myself with both Strength and love so that I can be in the world free and complete."

Reader: "That's really a great wish. Now, imagine what the outcome would be if your wish was granted. What would your life look like if you totally accepted yourself?"

Outcome

Querent's Outcome: Being able to live life comfortably. To be able to meet any challenges with confidence while treating myself with affection, self-worth, and kindness.

Nine of Cups, Nine of Pentacles, and the Empress

Reader: "Okay, now please tell me how these cards describe the outcome that you imagine for yourself."

Querent: "I see myself feeling as if I have everything I need. I can go after goals in my life knowing that I deserve it. The woman with all her coins reminds me that I am enough. The Empress reminds me that I need to also mother myself ,which is another reminder that I deserve all the good things that life can bring: a harvest."

The next two steps in the spread are cards that are pulled from a facedown position. Also, the reader takes on the role of interpreting what she sees while the querent listens.

Obstacle

Five of Swords, the Lovers, and Ten of Swords

Reader: "The Five of Swords, the Lovers, and Ten of Swords tells me a story. Perhaps it is an old one. But it makes me wonder, were you ever abandoned by someone?"

Querent: "I've been single since my divorce ten years ago. I just never got over that he cheated on me. He told me some really mean things that I never forgot, and it really made me feel bad about myself."

Reader: "It sounds like his rejection of you kicked off you beginning to reject yourself. Does that sound right?"

Querent: "Wow, yeah, I think that's right."

Reader: "Can you put your inner obstacle into one sentence starting with "My inner obstacle?"

Querent: "My inner obstacle is my self-rejection which stems from being abandoned."

Reader: "That is really good work. Now, can you make a sentence that is: your inner obstacle + 'is the obstacle that keeps me from' + your outcome?"

Querent: "My self-rejection stemming from being abandoned is the obstacle that keeps me from being able to live life comfortably, and to be able to meet any challenges with confidence while treating myself with affection, self-worth, and kindness."

Reader: "This is so powerful! Now, let's pull cards for your plan. Your plan is what you need to do in order to rewrite or defeat your inner obstacle."

Plan

Ace of Pentacles, the Star, and the Sun

Reader: "You have three golden discs in the sky. All three are radiant, they are seen by many. They are unapologetic and they shine. The Ace of Pentacles often indicates a reward, a gift from the Universe; it can also signal how you yourself are a gift from the Universe to others.

"The Star indicates taking a positive and inspirational mindset and allowing space for good things. And it is possible for good things to happen once again. Finally, we have the Sun, one of the most positive cards in the deck. For me, the Sun means "YES!" in the most succinct way possible.

"Here we see a change of mindset from being rejected and self-rejection to radical acceptance. Since the obstacle stems from another person rejecting you, the answer lies in you accepting others. We accept others by building relationships of all kinds, repairing friendships and family relationships, bringing new people into your life, and following your passions. What just makes you happy and how can you find others who share that happiness?

"Do you have a robust social network?"

Querent: "Not really. Mostly I work and just keep to myself."

Reader: "So can you formulate a one to two sentence plan from what I have shared so far?"

Querent: "Okay, here goes; I need to repair and build relationships of all kinds. I need to put myself out there and start doing things that bring me happiness and begin to cultivate friends who are also made happy by similar things. I need to change my mindset from rejected and self-rejecting to accepting and self-accepting."

Reader: "The last part is to pull it all together by saying, 'My wish is (__). When I plan to (__) then the outcome of (__) becomes possible.'"

Querent: "My wish is to accept myself just as I am. When I plan to make time for the hobbies that I enjoy and as I put myself out there to cultivate like-minded friends, then the outcome of being able to live life comfortably and meet any challenges with confidence while treating myself with affection, self-worth, and kindness is possible."

12

Judgement Is a Card, Not a Reading Style

You are a judger. We all are. As a reader, you will judge your querent. You will judge the cards, you will judge the question, and you will dispense your readings with bias. We cannot ever escape our subjective perspective. With observation and a willingness to be honest with yourself, however, you can use that subjectivity to inform the way you read tarot. It also makes you a better reader because when you are mindful of your subjectivity, you can give your querents two incredibly important things: agency within the reading and consent.

Querents often ask deeply vulnerable questions. They may be in an emotionally fragile place. They come to us looking for answers, sometimes to very difficult questions. Since we are being put in the role of authority, we have a responsibility to do the best we can. If we are not mindful, we can actually cause more harm than good.

Taking a walk through a psychic fair, you can easily hear snippets of other readers' sessions with querents. Even with this casual exploration, you can get a sense of how differently readers operate and how those differences affect their readings. You can also see many examples of plainly bad readings.

One thing I have noticed is how some readers seem to give opinions that are in no way related to the cards on the table. Sometimes, these opinions are delivered in a harsh or dismissive way, in a tone that clearly conveys that they have heard it all before and this querent is no different. I have also heard querents later in the food court or perusing the gemstone kiosks, telling their friends, "I felt like she was just giving me her opinion and not actually reading the cards."

These observations point to a disconnect between what the readers thought they were providing and what the querents actually wanted. The querents wanted a reading from the cards as transmitted and interpreted by the reader. There was a point, however, where the querent felt the reader leaned into territory that was too personal or too subjective. The querent wanted an oracle but got Aunt Karen instead.

Are We Always Right?

If we think we and our readings are always right because they come from Spirit, how can we ever learn and evolve? Where is the space to accept feedback and criticism? The problem with always being right is that we stop centering the session on the querent. Once we stop centering on the querent, we take away their agency. Unfortunately, this unexamined style of reading is not uncommon. Here are a few samples based on things I have heard over the years:

- As a confident reader, I simply approach the situation with the mindset of "I am not wrong."
- About 99 percent of the time, I feel I am not wrong because I get so "in the zone." I trust my gods as well as myself.
- Since I am an oracle, what comes out isn't mine so I don't filter it.

There is a type of cognitive bias called the overconfidence bias which is the tendency to lend too much weight to our own capabilities, especially if we are only internalizing praise and discounting any criticism. Overconfidence keeps us from becoming better readers because we resist any information that might help us change or grow. If we place ourselves as self-appointed gurus, we make readings about ourselves, not our querents. If our querents take issue with what we say in a reading or are harmed by it, we say it is their problem, not ours. This type of thinking is deeply harmful both to our querents (toward whom we have a responsibility) and to ourselves as readers.

To be fair, it takes an incredible amount of confidence to read for others and be out in public with our craft. Indeed, when society believes that what we do is a sham or ridiculous, we can inadvertently overcorrect. We can become too defensive of our skills. We may stand by our readings too fiercely rather than admit that we are wrong. We may also tend to give a reading that was more judgment than insight.

Things That Like to Barge in on Readings

Assumption

Every human on the planet makes instant, unconscious knee-jerk assumptions based on how someone looks or what they are wearing. What someone looks like or what they wear can influence your opinion about them and move the reading in the wrong direction. Note that your assumptions are not true—they are narratives built from your own experience and history. Don't lean in to these assumptions to shape your reading.

Opinion

Are you stating your opinion about the question in the reading? Are you saying what you are seeing in the cards, or are you riffing? Are you self-aware enough to know what the difference feels like? It is perfectly normal to have opinions about things that come up in sessions, but should they really be shared? If you do express your opinion, where does that opinion come from? Your wisdom, your experience, your bias, or something else? Understanding where the opinion is coming from helps you determine whether it is helpful to share or not.

Speculation

Are you drawing a conclusion based on the evidence? Are you speculating to fill in blanks that may appear in the reading, or to answer a question your querent is asking? Do you make it clear to your querent that what you are offering is a speculation and not the cards themselves?

Storytelling

One particularly tricky technique is to pay attention to what stories come up for you as you are reading for your querent. These personal stories may be an intuitive hit; you are being shown something from your own life that can add meaning to the reading. This technique needs to be used with caution, however, because once your story is shared, it can force the narrative of the querent's path onto your own. You might erroneously assume how a situation will progress, or you might cherry-pick the cards on the table to fit the narrative you have in mind. Even if you have heard the same question a million times, the story in response to that question from the reading is spectacularly unique to that querent. Take care not to pigeonhole someone's story through the lens of your own experience.

Being Triggered

Are you being triggered by the querent or by the question in some way that may interfere with your ability to read for them from a neutral standpoint? Does their question make you feel unsafe or bring up unpleasant thoughts or memories? When this happens, do you honor that and release the querent from the session because you cannot be a faithful messenger in that context?

Countertransference

Is there something about the querent that you respond to, whether you know why or not? Are you being overly helpful or disclosing too much about yourself, or are you more critical and judgmental of the querent? When you notice this, are you honest with yourself? Do you take appropriate measures to process your own issues so that countertransference doesn't interfere with the session? And if you cannot, do you end the session with the querent?

Common Sense Approaches to Keep Your Judgment in Check

Self-Monitoring

You have to pay as much attention to yourself during a session as you do the cards and querent. The sooner you can identify and deal with thoughts that are biased and speculative, the quicker you can get on track or end the reading if it isn't working for you. This is the absolute opposite of the "everything that flies out of my mouth is okay" mindset.

Clear Communication

Make it very clear that what you have to say has a source other than the tarot reading. A distinct separation between strictly reading the cards and information that comes from you from other sources (psychic, personal, etc.) has to be maintained at all times. "I am getting this intuitively. It is not in the cards," or "Can I give you a word of advice as a mom of four kids, too?" Make it clear.

Consent

Always ask your querent before sharing a story. "Do you mind if I give you a quick story that I think illustrates your journey right now?" or "May I put my 'big sister' hat on for a sec?" Always get their permission.

Querent Agency

Deeply listen and watch your querent. They may be saying yes but their body language may be telling you no. If you sense any discomfort (especially non-verbally), do not proceed. If your querent says no, that they just want you to read the cards, take it in stride. They are giving you feedback about what they want. They hired you as a tarot card reader first, not an opinion and advice dispenser who sometimes reads the cards.

Sample Reading: What Went Wrong and How to Make It Right

"I was reading for a friend, though we are not talking to each other at the moment. I know I am not supposed to judge, but she kept asking questions about this married guy at work and it made me feel uneasy. I tried to change the session to be more about her own marriage, but she didn't want that. Eventually, I just shut down. I told her I couldn't do any more questions about a possible affair. I guess reading tarot isn't for me. I wonder if I just lost a friend, too."

What Went Wrong?

The Reader Became Triggered

While the reader is saying she is not supposed to judge the querent she did exactly that: she says that the questions made her feel uneasy. Why would they make her feel uneasy? Because she believes it is wrong.

The Reader Kept Going

The reader did not acknowledge her own discomfort and instead decided to plow ahead despite her deep reservations. She did not honor her own boundaries. We know that because the questions came one after another, and she let it go on too long in an attempt to please the reader at her own discomfort.

The Reader Changed the Reading Without Consent

The reader (rather sanctimoniously, I might add) finally decided that what the querent really needed was to forget about that possible affair partner and work on her marriage instead. As you can see, the querent wasn't having it.

The Reader Did Not Give the Querent What She Wanted

The querent wanted a reading about the actual, but the reader decided that what the querent really needed was a reading on the psychological. Basically, the reader did not uphold the three things I always advocate: communication, consent, and querent agency. She also put up her boundaries way too late.

How Could This Reading Have Gone Right?
The Reader Needed to Check In with Herself

"I am uncomfortable with this. Can I move forward as a neutral reader, or do I need to end the session?"

End the Session If She Could Not Read Objectively

"I am sorry, but I am not going to be able to do a reading on this topic. I am just not getting the information (or, "I don't do third-party readings," or "I am just not able to make the connection").

> **Reader's Tip**
> Ending the session is not a failure on your part; it is actively watching for your bias and not proceeding when it is prudent to walk away. Your own boundaries may shift and grow over time, and that is perfectly okay too.

Proceed with the Session While Telling the Querent Very Clearly What You Can and Cannot Do

We present our boundaries, then allow our querents to make the choice. Consent at every single step of the way is the key. Communicate and get permission.

Answer the Querent's Question If You Proceed

Many newer readers default to a more psychological style of reading when it is not appropriate. If a querent is asking how she can make rent this month, answer that. Do not rewrite the question to be some version of, "What is my psychological stance on the nature of money?" If you find yourself veering off into psychoanalysis land when your querent just wants to know if they are about to get evicted, it means you are not listening. It could also mean you are not trusting that the cards are answering the question. You are taking the power away from the querent.

Reader's Tip

I think this is more the exception than the rule, but if this does happen, again we stick to communication and consent. "The reading is talking about something else. I guess it wants to get this topic out of the way. Is it okay for me to proceed here?" Once they say yes, proceed.

As a reader, you can still have boundaries on what you will read on— you don't have to read for anyone about anything. You can be a reader who won't do certain questions, and that is totally okay. It is also possible that your boundaries may change over time; they often do when you read for a lot of people over a long period of time. As a reader for others, I have become less judgmental of people's paths and more understanding about the nature of complex human relationships. But if something does affect me to the point that I know I cannot be the best reader for a client, I tell them and end the session.

Card Bias

Up until now, we've talked about judgment from the reader's perspective— ways in which the querent or the question are judged and how those judgements present themselves. Another factor in this equation is how we judge individual cards within tarot and how those judgments might keep us from reading the cards as clearly as we can. Each and every one of us has innate biases; some cards are our favorites, and others we dislike. These innate reactions are basically us as readers transferring our emotions and feelings onto the cards. These internal models can influence the message we share with our querents. Here is a story to illustrate what I mean.

I was once friends with a fellow tarot reader, but we had a falling out. I was following her on social media and saw that she posted about the Queen of Wands. At the time, "Queen of Wands" was the name of my business.

Her write up of Queen of Wands was particularly nasty. According to her, the Queen of Wands was a drama queen who loved to stir up chaos and make everything about her. While that may be some of who the Queen of Wands is, that is not *all* she is; it was clear that my ex-friend had transferred her dislike of me onto the Queen of Wands card.

While she had a right to her opinion, her bias would be totally unfair to any other unsuspecting person who also shows up in a reading as the Queen of Wands card. Or, say a querent asks about a hot date and the Queen of Wands appears. What would my ex-friend say? Probably not too many good things. Her obvious hangup about the Queen of Wands indicates two things: that she needs to be mindful of her bias bleeding into her readings, and the cards can indicate areas for personal growth and self-discovery.

My ex-friend's response is not an uncommon one. Some cards just trigger readers more. I remember very clearly hearing a reader tell a querent that Knight of Swords was "always an abusive type." Poor Knight of Swords! I've also seen plenty of readers clearly indicate dislike of other characters such as the Emperor and the Hierophant. Of course, these are responses that may be traumatic in origin. Perhaps they are fighting the patriarchy every day or left an autocratic abuser. But the Emperor is just as good and necessary as the Empress. The Hierophant is just as helpful and incredible as the High Priestess. If we find that we cannot see each card from a place of considered neutrality, we are doing a disservice to the reading. We are putting our spin on it rather than letting the reading speak for itself.

The good news is that we can do much to build a better relationship to each of our tarot archetypes. In doing so, we work out some of our own stuff along the way. We as readers are not only helping others but are helping ourselves through the act of reading for others, too. It is a win-win situation for everyone involved. As with any relationship, your connection to these seventy-eight cards will grow over time. If your practice becomes static and stale and you always see the same cards in the same ways with little variation, then it is time to shake things up a bit. The activity at the end of this chapter should help if you find yourself struggling with some cards.

Activity
Don't Hate the Hierophant—
How to Build New Relationships with Difficult Cards

Find a card you have difficulty with. Perhaps you don't know why you have difficulty with that card, or you have difficulty with a card everyone else loves. Perhaps the difficulty isn't obvious—you don't dislike the card per se, but you just can't seem to feel comfortable when it shows up in a reading. Once you have chosen your card, free-write (I suggest a good, healthy two pages or so) answering these questions:

★ What emotions come up for me when you appear?
★ When I look at you, I focus on these aspects of your image and I think it might mean …
★ You remind me of …
★ You show up when …

Once you have written your pages, leave the assignment for twenty-four hours. During that time, notice if anything comes up for you: any memories, dreams, or situations with others that show up in your life. Feel free to write this all down.

After twenty-four hours, pull out your free-write pages and compare them to your life over the last twenty-four hours. Were there some themes that made themselves clear both on the pages and in your life? Did you have any dreams that connected to the themes you shared on your page?

Reading through your free-writing, underline sentences and words that feel particularly relevant to you and put them in their own list. You should have a list of especially powerful words and sentences regarding your interaction with your card thus far.

Now take the card out of your deck. If you have multiple decks, choose the card that triggers you the least or doesn't look like how you naturally associate with that card. Place it upright so you can look at the image and connect with it for this next part.

Imagine that you are the person or aspect within the card. Really try to visualize yourself as that card. Once you feel you have embodied the card, go through the list of responses you wrote earlier and write a rebuttal or explanation from the card you are now embodying.

An Example

Free-write passage: The Hierophant is harsh, closed-minded, and judgmental.

The Hierophant: My role is to facilitate others through their own relationship to God. I love God so completely that I made many sacrifices in order to be a servant to his will. This includes serving the poor, the abandoned, and the weak. Every day, I work on being humble, which includes listening for God's voice everywhere. Wherever love is, I want to be there too.

There is no right or wrong way to do this exercise; your card will speak with and through you to process and integrate the archetype into a centered whole. Keep going until you feel a shift and watch for how that shift shows up in readings moving forward.

13

How They Mishear What You Say and Why

Every reader has been there at some point—you are laying out the cards, your question is strong, and the narrative appears before you as clear as day. You are conveying the message, and you know deep in your soul that the reading is accurate. But then your querent pulls back, folds her arms, and says that you are wrong. As readers, we can usually tell when a reading is off. Maybe the question was not right, the spread didn't quite work, or you were just not vibing with your querent for some reason.

This chapter is focused on identifying and explaining why something is going wrong in the reading. The next chapter, "What to Do When a Reading Goes Wrong," is where I lay out what to do when these sessions are hijacked. As you go through this chapter, think about reading situations that seemed similar and what you did about it. If you have not yet read for someone, you can apply these situations to something else that has happened in your life.

When People Shoot the Messenger

You might wonder why someone comes back for the same reading with the same question over and over again while ignoring the cards' advice. Why do querents put words in your mouth, claiming that you said things you never said? When these things happen, they can really mess with your confidence and sense of self-worth as a reader. We end up questioning our reading skills and maybe even put away our decks as a result. There is a huge responsibility to shoulder when we become readers, but the responsibility is only partly ours.

I can't tell you how many times I've read for one person in a group setting where the querent was shaking her head "no" while her friends were all nodding emphatically "yes." I remember doing a live gallery reading (a reading for a large group of people in a public setting). One young woman asked about her love life, and it didn't look great. As gently as I could, I delivered the news while her friends were about to jump out of their seats in agreement. The greater audience was also on board with the message. After I delivered my reading she said, "Oh, that's fine, I don't believe in this stuff anyway." The poor thing caused an uproar as the rest of the crowd jumped to defend my reading (and to defend themselves, since they were believers!) So if we are doing sessions and our querents tell us we are wrong, should we believe them? Not necessarily.

As a reader, you may also find yourself as the unwitting scapegoat in other people's relationship dynamics. People want to have a fall guy. "I am leaving you because my reader said you were no good." Your readings (and by extension, you) become the "out" when people want to deflect responsibility for their own actions. As a professional reader, I have had angry exes get a reading and basically use the time to tell me that I was the cause of the breakup. Or they use me as a way to gather intel about their partner. If you suspect that you and your reading are being weaponized, end the session. And yes, even if you read casually for friends and family, it can still happen to you. In fact, this is a greater danger when reading for those close to you. Will your friend still be your friend if the reading suggested that she break up with her boyfriend but she decides to stay? Is she going to invite you over for dinner with said boyfriend there after she told him about your reading? Before you do readings for friends and family, deeply consider whether it will affect your relationship with them.

When Querents Cannot Hear What You Are Saying

Another way that querents may tell us we are wrong (when we are actually right) happens when they become so focused on one thing that they are incapable of hearing anything except for the one particular answer they are looking for. For example, I remember telling someone in a reading that I saw a family connection to Utah that felt like it was during the 1800s. She shook her head and told me she had no idea what I was talking about. Then, later that evening,

I overheard her mention how she recently found out that she had Mormon ancestry. Incredulous, I asked her, "How did you not see that what I was saying was connected to this?" She said that it just hadn't occurred to her.

Sometimes querents are so focused on looking for the word "blue" that they totally miss it when you say "cobalt." There can be a focus or particularity to a querent's listening ear that can be quite myopic at times. You weren't wrong, you just didn't say it using the specific words this person needed in order to get it.

So what the hell is going on with all of this? How do we readers understand what is in play and how to handle it? In a word: psychology. In any reading session, there are multiple things happening at the same time. This is not easy, but don't panic! I am going to give you a very basic guide to different psychological terms that will help you identify what is happening when it happens, and how you can best deal with it when it comes up.

Transference

Transference is a term first coined by Sigmund Freud. It is basically a phenomenon where someone transfers how they might respond to one person (say, their father) onto someone else (their therapist). Transference doesn't just happen in therapy; it occurs between people all of the time. In readings your querents may transfer how they feel about someone in their life to you. If you are reading for people you already know, this is usually less of an issue, but if you are a reader for hire, you are like a blank slate—upon which a querent can write whatever they want.

One type of transference to be particularly careful about is *guru transference,* where your querent will assign to you a wisdom or spiritual significance that is not, in fact, based in reality. They will hang on every word you say and place you on a pedestal. But if you make a mistake in front of them like drop an f-bomb, burp, or otherwise show your very human side, they can't handle it.

When you are placed on a pedestal, you will eventually fall, and hard. When you notice this happening, do your best to center the adulation on tarot, not on you as the tarot reader. Stop a reading if you sense that the querent is beginning to over-rely upon them. Rewrite any questions that begin with, "Should I?" to questions that come from a place of agency.

Another type of transference is *romantic transference*. The work you put into giving a reading can be deeply intimate, and your querent may confuse your kindness and listening skills for romantic interest. This is particularly true of querents who generally have difficulty in the love department. If you find that you have a querent who is crushing on you hardcore, stop seeing them for a while. Make it clear that your only role in their life is to be their reader.

Finally, there are transferences where a querent responds to you as if you were another *authority figure* in their lives—and usually it is an authority figure they do not like! Perhaps they start treating you like their mom who nags them all the time or like a sibling who just thinks she is better than everyone else. Transference is largely unconscious, so if you find yourself wondering why you are being treated in a way that doesn't seem to connect to your work, transference may be at play.

If you read for someone and tell them their abusive boyfriend is bad news but then they stop talking to you as a result, they have transferred some kind of shame or judgment they carry about the relationship onto you. Instead of being angry with the right person, they transfer that onto you. This is why I recommend caution for certain types of readings among friends and family.

Projection

Projection, a term first coined by Freud, is the psychological phenomenon where people will attribute to another what is true about themselves. For example, a cheater in a relationship may become irrationally suspicious about their partner and accuse them of stepping out, in effect totally projecting onto someone else what they themselves are doing.

In readings, projection can manifest as accusations of you having an agenda you simply do not have. I've had querents tell me things that made no sense to me at all, like one querent who told me that she was sick of my games. Huh? I literally talked to her once a year. What was she talking about? Whatever was going on within her was thrown onto me.

I can typically tell I am working with a projection issue when the cards are not supporting the querent's narrative. For example, a querent may say that her ex isn't a good parent and is looking for a reading to confirm her suspicions. When you pull the cards, though, you see that the reading shows that the ex is actually a good parent. You get no cards that are confirming her judgment. But if you do a reading on her as a parent, you may see the cards for her that you thought would go to him!

Reader's Tip

Dealing with projection in a reading is difficult because the querent wants to be validated—namely, they want you to tell them they are right. Remember that your job is to read the cards, and if those cards do not agree with your querent, you need to tell them so. However, you can also lead the session where the focus is on providing the best outcomes. In the case of the above example, I might ask to follow up with a reading on what the querent needs to know about her children or about how she can be the best mom for them right now.

Cognitive Distortions

"Cognitive distortion" is an umbrella term for thoughts and beliefs we may have that are often illogical. These distortions act like a broken pane of glass: they keep a person from being able to truly see the reading as it is. Being able to identify cognitive distortions when you see them will help you by giving you the space you need to step back. If you don't take the distortion personally, you can eventually help them step around their distortions so they can hear the reading as you intend it. A great resource for this is the seminal book on the topic, *Feeling Good: The New Mood Therapy* by David D. Burns. Below is a list of some of the most common cognitive distortions I encounter and what I do when a querent is in the midst of one.

All or Nothing Thinking

People often turn to tarot because they want clarity, which usually means definitive answers: yes or no, go or stay. So if a reading is more nuanced or adds layers of complexity to a situation, a querent might try to force a clearer answer than is necessarily there. This desire comes from a place of anxiety— they want their anxiety relieved and only a clear answer will do.

Querents in this situation may try to push you to come to a conclusion that you do not see. They will often ask detail-oriented questions delivered in rapid-fire succession. It may feel like you are suddenly on the witness stand being cross-examined. You may find yourself on your back foot just trying to keep up or even jumping to conclusions just to take the pressure off. These situations are really tough. You might be able to read on some clarifying questions to try to get more details, but ultimately your role here is to stand firm in what you are seeing and not force a reading to be what the querent wishes it to be.

Overgeneralizing

This cognitive distortion occurs when someone sees one piece of negative information and then makes a conclusion that it is true for everything else. Here is an example of how I see this show up in readings.

> *Reader:* "I see in this reading that you have made some great shifts in how you approach love, but the short-term prediction shows someone appearing who will have some of the same narcissistic traits as your ex that you will need to navigate."
>
> *Querent:* "But I have worked so hard to make positive changes! I guess I am just doomed. I will never be happy in love."

Overgeneralizing tends to happen when someone is frustrated and feels despair. This often happens with querents who expect the reading to give them something to hope for. This is a legitimate desire, especially if we have been working really hard to make positive changes. We want to see that our effort is going to be rewarded. So, when a reading shows negativity down the road, we may feel doomed by assigning that one negative future experience as the Universe's answer to our plight.

Reader's Tip

Fight overgeneralizing with specificity and personal responsibility. Help them take despair and turn it into opportunity. "What is the lesson from this one instance? What do I need to know to help me pass this test? What are the signs from the Universe when I am on the right path?" Remind them that readings are course corrections more than they are final answers.

Filtering

Filtering is the distortion where negative information is given more weight than positive information. I see it most commonly when querents only focus on negative cards while ignoring all the positive cards in a reading.

> *Reader:* "I pulled the Sun, the Tower, the Star, and Ten of Pentacles. As you can see, buying a house will eventually work out but it will be a wild ride to get there."
>
> *Querent:* "Oh my god, but what do you think that Tower card actually means? Could it mean that my real estate agent pulls out? Or maybe I will lose a house I actually want? This is terrible! The Tower is horrible, right?"
>
> *Reader:* "But you are forgetting that you also got the Sun, the Star, and Ten of Pentacles! All these cards indicate that you are going to have a great outcome!"
>
> *Querent:* "Yeah but what do you think the Tower really means, though?"

When a querent is filtering and fixating on a negative card, they are cherry-picking the reading and ignoring your delivery. Some people's anxiety ramps up into hypervigilance from relatively innocuous data because they are always scanning the horizon for the next bad thing they need to worry about. This is often a trauma response, so be compassionate.

It is helpful to get querents dealing with this distortion to see the whole reading in the larger perspective. I remind my querents that each tarot card is weighted equally; "bad" cards such as Death or the Tower are not inherently more powerful than the Sun or the Lovers card.

The power of a reading comes from the narrative; it doesn't make sense to just pull one card from a spread in isolation and give it more emotional weight than it is ultimately worth. I deal with filtering by asking a querent to trust my interpretation. I reassure them by telling them I am not hiding anything, and if I thought there was something to worry about, I would tell them. Remind your querent that you are on their side to read the whole reading and focus on the outcome.

Reader's Tip
One powerful and simple technique I use is to take the spread and put it into two piles, one of "good" cards, the other of "bad" cards to easily show just how big each pile is. This technique helps them see the greater context and tone of the reading.

Ultimately, filtering can be hard to navigate. I do not recommend predictive tarot readings for some people because any kind of negative news (even the kind that is ultimately helpful) triggers worry, anxiety, and even panic attacks. For these kinds of querents, a more clarifying type of reading or even an oracle card reading might be more beneficial. It's best to use gentle cards for these querents.

Magnification

Similar to filtering, querents exhibiting this kind of cognitive distortion weigh negative information far more heavily than is necessary. This is also known as catastrophizing or making a mountain out of a molehill. For example, every time the Death card appears, it usually elicits the question, "Does this mean that I/my spouse/my parent/my pet is going to die soon?" Well no, because we were asking about a promotion at work.

The best way I have found to tackle this distortion is to encourage questions and dialogue. If the reading is a one-way street with you doing all the talking (many querents will indeed fully expect that you do all the talking), then you will not be able to gauge how they are taking in the information. Make sure that after a reading you are asking questions, such as "How does this sit with you?" or "What do you think about what is shared here?" Allowing space for feedback in the reading allows you to ascertain whether what you shared and what they heard are on the same page.

Dialoging is really important because magnification will often cause querents to put words in my mouth. They will claim that I said things that I know for a fact I never said at all. It boggles my mind how people remember a reading versus how I remember it. The greater their cognitive distortion, the bigger the difference will be. By asking questions to ascertain what they've heard, you can make sure that the reading is being conveyed in the way that you mean it.

Disqualifying the Positive

Disqualifying the positive is the cognitive distortion where someone never gives credit to the positive things in their lives. I see this in querents who may be stuck in "victim thinking." You can sense this distortion is active when the querent monologues about their past and the difficulties in their lives but resists suggestions to fix the problems. They decline to feel gratitude toward what is good and working for them and avoid attempts to help them see the good things in their life.

These querents tend to hijack a reading the most. You may find that you can barely get a word in and that you are being pushed into playing the role of witness or bystander to their perceived plight. Any attempts you make to redirect them to the positives or to a reading that emphasizes their personal accountability is ignored. I find this kind of cognitive distortion one of the most challenging to work through. You are basically being manipulated into either playing into their distortion by agreeing with them or relegated to being a bad person like all the other bad people in their life.

Reader's Tip

Sometimes you will find that you are being used more as a sounding board while the advice and support you are delivering through tarot go unheeded. If that is the case, decide what role you want to play as their reader. Do you allow them to position you into the role of playing audience to their perpetual victimhood and negativity? Remember that you have the right to directly engage them by telling them what your approach is. If that is not a fit, it is okay to let them go.

Emotional Reasoning

Oh boy, you know all those twin flame/soulmate readings where the partner is absolute trash but your querent is telling you that they feel like they "met their destiny" when they are with them? Chalk most of that up to the emotional reasoning distortion.

With emotional reasoning, any way you feel about a situation must be objectively true. It can be incredibly dangerous when it comes to romantic relationships because it can trap people into thinking that chemistry is a reliable indicator for a healthy and compatible match or that chemistry is the only thing that matters.

Querents who want a reading about romantic entanglements like this are often looking for two things: they want confirmation that what they feel has a higher meaning or purpose greater than the red flags that often come with the relationship, and part of them knows that what they are feeling may not be right, so they need help to see the real situation for what it really is. The hard part for you, dear reader, is determining which of these your querent is.

Reader's Tip

Tread with caution. Querents with a strong habit of emotional reasoning are the most likely to lash out at you if you tell them something they do not want to hear. Their reaction is very similar to an addict flying into a rage when someone throws out their stash.

Fallacy of Change

"If only he'd change, then we could be happy." This is, as you can guess, a common distortion in readings. This distortion is the dog whistle for dysfunctional relationships. It is common for a querent with this distortion to expect that a reading will predict when the other person will finally change. It often appears in love readings where a querent invested time and energy in helping that person reach their potential, but that potential hasn't materialized. Now getting impatient, the querent seeks a reading about how to get their partner to change. Many codependent and enabling relationships fall under this pattern. It is also related to the sunk cost fallacy, i.e., "But I have already put so much into this relationship."

Reader's Tip

With these kinds of readings, I try a couple of approaches. First, I might suggest doing a reading on the *question*: "What does this look like if they are unable to make the changes that I require?" I might also turn it around by asking, "What do I need to change within myself in order to make this work, assuming they do not change at all; will I be happy with this scenario?" In most cases, querents with this fallacy in play start their reading with, "Should I stay or should I go?"

Fallacy of Fairness

When we are suffering, we often say things like "Why me?" or, "I am a good person, why is this happening to me?" But you know what I never hear? "I won the lottery! Why is this happening to me?" We only ask about fairness when we are on the losing end of the equation. We ask this question because on some level, we believe that the Universe works as a meritocracy. Since we are good people, surely good things will happen to us. But when bad things happen, it's not fair!

As readers, we might be able to definitively tell querents why this unfair thing happened to them. We can also help put things into perspective so that they don't see the situation as a personal slight from the Universe. Karma was not involved; God is not doling out a punishment. Life is just really unfair sometimes, so we need to handle the pain we are going through and find ways to move forward with resilience rather than bitterness.

Activity
Identify the Distortion—
A Mini Pop Quiz of Scenarios from Real-Life Readings

Following are some examples loosely based on real readings I have conducted. What distortions do you see? Keep in mind that more than one could be at play. Identify the distortions and write a script for how you would move the reading forward and help your querent see past their distortion.

Scenario #1

Querent: "I've been single for a few years, when will someone new come into my life?"

Reader: "I pulled the following cards for you: the Hermit, Two of Swords, Eight of Cups, Ten of Wands, and Three of Cups. What this indicates is that you have been alone and stuck—doing the same thing and expecting different results. If you are willing to work hard to get out of your comfort zone, you will be rewarded with a renewed social life. I do not see love just yet, but I think this reading emphasizes relearning to walk before you run. The Three of Cups tells me that you are successful in making changes you need to initiate in your life to begin the process of transformation which, I think, will take you to love down the road."

Querent: "But you don't see love in the cards?"

Reader: "Not at this time."

Querent: "I guess I am just doomed to never be loved. I'll be alone forever. Nothing ever changes."

Scenario #2

Querent: "My good buddy from way back is about to launch a startup. It's in an industry that is new to the both of us, but I just have such a good feeling about it. I'm sure that if I cash out my retirement to invest, I am just going to make bags of money. Honestly, I don't even know why I am here getting a reading about it. I mean, I am pretty intuitive and everything in my gut is just telling me that this is so right."

Reader: "I pulled the Knight of Swords, the World, Ten of Swords, and Eight of Cups for you. What I see here is that you start off really strong. The Knight of Swords speaks to the sureness of your actions and how assertive you both are to get this venture off the ground. You successfully launch the start-up into the world, but that Ten of Swords indicates that your wings are clipped just as you reach cruising altitude; it could indicate a heavy financial loss. Finally, the Eight of Cups speaks to you walking away with significant losses incurred."

Querent: "This is just a prediction and predictions can change, right? I mean, a reading can be wrong. I just feel that this is going to be a huge success. My buddy and I have already invested so much so far. Sorry, but this reading just isn't resonating for me."

Scenario #3

Querent: "I have an interview next week. Will I get the job?"

Reader: "How exciting! Let's see. I am looking at the High Priestess, Ace of Wands, Four of Pentacles reversed, and Strength reversed. I think you will get a job offer. The Ace of Wands to me is a large indicator of an offer. But that Four of Pentacles and Strength reversed tell me that the offer package is not exactly what you are looking for. Strength reversed is specifically telling me that you do not have much negotiating power to change this."

Querent: "But, is there anything I can do to get the package I want?"

Reader: "I believe that the final two cards are indicating strongly that there isn't much you can do."

Querent: "Can you pull a few more cards specifically asking if there is anything I can do?"

Reader: "Sure. Here are the Wheel of Fortune, the Moon, and the Fool. I think there will be some back and forth negotiations, but that Moon is not a positive indicator. Actually, when I see both the Moon and the Fool together, they tell me that this company intends to slow-walk your negotiating process while they seek out someone with less experience who will take the job."

Querent: "But what if I talk to my friend who works there? I really want this job, and I really need the salary to be good. Isn't there any way we can get them to come in higher?"

14
What to Do When a Reading Goes Wrong

When I first started reading, I was exhilarated. People told me that the readings were accurate, and I loved getting all of that good feedback. But eventually there came a time where something just didn't work and I didn't know how to fix it.

I have come to understand that most of the challenges have to do with these themes: expectations, psychological triggers, communication, and boundaries. Most of these can be easily resolved once we know where the problem stems from. And the good news is that most of these problems are not because you are a bad reader!

What follows is a list of common challenges readers might face and solutions to those problems. Some will be familiar to you already because they were covered in the last chapter, although this is the chapter where I talk about how you, the reader, can best deal with it.

We then follow up with an activity that is built just for you so that when these things happen (and they will), you have a tool up your sleeve that can help you regain confidence, fast. Now, let's get into it!

Querents Who Arrive in a Crisis

If a querent shows up in panic mode, the first question I ask myself is, "Is the querent in a place where they can be receptive to a reading?" Are they able to hear what a reading might say, or are they so emotional they are talking nonstop between sobs? The absolute first thing you need to do is a wellness check. Ask these questions:

- Are you hurt?
- Are you safe?
- Are you considering hurting yourself?

Depending on the answers, you may end up calling the police or a crisis hotline. Don't play hero and try to fix something above your "pay grade" as a reader. Call the appropriate people who can best help.

Reader's Tip

It is always a good idea to have a list of crisis numbers relevant to your geographic location. Keep a handy reference sheet for numbers that include emergency services, domestic violence services, homeless shelters, free legal aid, and food banks as a start. If you suspect that your querent is unable to keep the presence of mind to do this for her or himself, offer to be present as they make the call. While you are not a social worker, you can still be instrumental in helping querents get to the place or people who can help them best.

Querents Who Arrive in a Panic

Some querents will show up upset and emotional. While a reading is not an emergency, the emotions they are feeling do feel urgent. If you have run through the wellness check and everything seems okay from a safety perspective, determine whether the querent needs to vent.

People who vent usually talk quickly and jump around in topics. Perhaps your role is to listen and validate feelings. You may also offer to breathe with them and have them slow down their pace to match yours. If listening and breathing has made them more receptive, you can move forward with the reading but if they are still tense and upset, it is a good idea to do the reading another time.

Querents with Mental Health Challenges

You may have querents whom you suspect are dealing with mental health issues. If this is the case, refer them to the appropriate agency that can help. If you have a querent who is using you in lieu of a therapist when they really need someone who is qualified as a therapist, do not let them see you as a proxy. If you are not trained to help treat depression, do not take on that role. Sometimes you may have to tell a querent that you can no longer see them because you are not the specialist they need; this is to protect them *and* you. It is possible that the querent will never see you again, and they may find another reader rather than get the help they need. While disappointing, their response is not your responsibility. Your responsibility is to know when you can be a reader for them and when what they need is beyond your scope. You have done the right thing by referring out.

Querents Who Reveal or Plan Something Harmful

A few years back, I read about a murderer who was brought to the police by a tarot reader. After murdering his flatmate, he went to her to get a reading. The reading began to reveal the crime and he broke down confessing what he had done. The reader called the emergency hotline, but thinking it was a joke, the police did not arrive until one hour later. She spent that whole hour trying to keep him there and talking while she waited for the police to arrive. They did, and it was through her efforts that the killer was caught without any more violence. This is an extreme case; in my own work, I have not been in any situations where I felt the need to call the police (thank all the gods). But as readers, there is a chance, however slight, that someone might reveal what they are thinking of doing or have committed an act that harms another. My philosophy is that I will not hesitate to call the police and give information about someone who confesses to a crime where someone was hurt or plans on hurting another. I will also call child protective services, or the elderly abuse hotline if my querent has confessed or tells me they plan to hurt or harm a child or elderly person.

I take protecting my querents' identity and the session's contents very seriously. Like a therapist, I will not tell anyone if a person has seen me or not. I am also fairly libertine about the goings-on of others; you do you, but when it comes to abuse, rape, assault, or murder I will not hesitate for a second to report it, and neither should you.

Querents Who Expect a Mind Reader

Some querents expect you to tell them what is on their mind without actually using their words and telling you. This is an issue of expectations: what they expect a reader to do and what most readers *can* do are not the same.

You will know that you have encountered this attitude when they won't give you questions when asked, or they will refuse to say too much because they are afraid of giving you "intel." They will say, "Oh, just whatever comes up." Don't fall for this trap—98 percent of the time there *is* something they want a reading on, but what they want even more is to know whether you will see it on your own. If you do, you will have passed their mind reading psychic "test," but this test isn't a good one. Being psychic is not the same as mind reading, nor does it mean that a reader will get a list in the order of the querent's priority. General readings don't always show whatever querents want them to show.

When I encounter these types and get that initial reluctance, I lay it out: "If you want a reading on something specific, you have to tell me up front. It may be a different style than what you are used to, but this is how I work. Please wait until after the session to determine whether you got what you came to see me for." They will often reluctantly follow your lead but then once they see how amazing you are as a reader, will loosen up.

Reader's Tip

Don't let a querent dictate to you how to conduct your own tarot session. Lay out your expectations and boundaries and let them choose whether they want to move forward. Do not change how you read to meet their expectations. Stand firm in your process.

Querents Who Want to Play the "Gotcha!" Game

While some querents test us because they have their own ideas about how tarot works, others test you because they are trying to play "Gotcha!" Their goal is to catch you being fake. They often do this by taking wedding rings off of fingers, lying, or asking intentionally vague or misleading questions to throw you off. I once did a reading for a querent at a public event. His question was, "How does my love life look?" It seemed like a vague question, but I was on the clock and only had a few minutes with each person. I didn't have time to work out a clearer question, so I went with it.

The reading screamed that he was married. But I assumed that he was single by how he worded the question. I felt like I was fighting the reading. After I told him what I saw he said, "Oh, that is interesting, because I am married."

I responded (very crossly, I might add), "Why didn't you tell me in the first place?" Once he said he was married, the whole reading fell into focus. I then gave him the updated reading that was there all along, yelling at me.

I dislike the song and dance someone wants to put me through in order to test me; in most cases, these tests actually mean this: "I assume that readers are liars and cons unless you prove it to me otherwise." Yikes, this is not how I want to work at all!

If you get the sense that someone is trying to play the Gotcha! game with you, don't play along. Demand specificity where they are playing in generalities. Call out readings if tarot is telling you more than what the querent is saying. And if they are being real jerks about it, end the session.

Reader's Tip

There is one caveat to someone being intentionally vague. Sometimes, a querent is afraid of telling you something. They may mention one thing hoping that another thing is not revealed. If this is the case, like with all things, communication and consent is how to proceed. Tell them, "I see something else going on here besides what you mentioned. Do you want me to talk about it?" From there, they can choose how they would like the reading to proceed.

Querents Who Are Comparison Shoppers

Some querents see a lot of different readers. They go from reader to reader with the same question. Reading for these kinds of querents can be challenging because they are often comparing you to other readers.

In sessions they might try to butter you up by saing, "Oh wow, you are so much better than that other reader." Or they might test you, saying things such as, "That other reader was so amazing, everything she said was 100 percent accurate but she moved out of the area." They might also try to get you to do a reading after they exhausted the last reader, "I just don't feel like that reader really told me what the real deal was." This is all manipulation, don't take any of it to heart.

If they mention another reader or reading and try to compare you to them, don't comment on it. In fact, tell them that you do not want to know. And if a querent seems hell-bent on taking you to task because the reading is not confirming what the last reader said, don't argue with them. You were not there, you did not see the cards, you don't know what was actually said.

Comparison shoppers are often hard to please; in part, this is why they keep looking and looking for the perfect reader or reading. But that perfect reader does not exist. Do the best you can, but don't try to "fix" what the other readers did for this person. Nor do you have to live up to the reader your querent has put on a pedestal. Do your best and stay out of the fray—next week, this querent will be on to another reader anyway.

Querents Who Talk a Lot in Session

People are talkative for a variety of reasons. Some talkers are lonely, others just don't know how to stop talking. Some people may need a therapist more than a reader but come to see you anyway. Some talkers love to interject their opinion or make a statement in between every sentence you utter. Whatever the reason, you need to navigate these people carefully because it is not an uncommon occurrence where a reader (after being interrupted quite a bit) gives up and lets the querent talk. And guess what? That querent may go to others and say, "Well, I don't know if she is a good reader because she barely gave me a reading!" How unfair is that, right?

What you can do is call out the behavior and give guidelines. Try doing it nicely. You can say something like, "It seems like you need someone to listen to you today…is that the role you would like me to play for you?" If it continues, you can be more firm (go ahead, it's okay to be direct): "I need you to stop talking so I can give you the reading you came to me for." Querents will be angrier that you let them talk (and they didn't get a reading) than if you told them firmly and politely to stop talking.

Next are the guidelines. "Please withhold commentary or questions until I finish. Then we can discuss what was revealed." You can even begin your session with these guidelines. You can explain that the commentary breaks your intuitive flow. Usually, once they understand what the expectations are, things go more easily.

When a Reading Is Not Connecting

Occasionally we will conduct a reading where the cards are suddenly talking to us in another language. It might feel like you are fighting the reading for crumbs while your querent is sitting there looking at you like you've lost your mind. It often just makes it worse if you continue. If you find this is happening, end the session. Don't try to push for it. Recall in chapter X, "Yes, You're Psychic" that pushing engages anxiety which is antithetical to the open and receptive place you need to be to conduct a good reading.

While the querent will no doubt be disappointed, it is better to try another day. A reading not connecting can mean that the two of you don't mesh, or they are someone who is hard to read for in general. Or maybe the planets are not in alignment—who knows? If you end the session with the querent, you can offer to read for them another day or see if there is someone else you know who can read for them. Once the session has ended, do a reading for yourself to find out what happened with this querent. Remember to use tarot for yourself as well as for others!

Querents Who Are Madly in Love with a Soul Mate, But Your Reading Tells You Something Else

Love readings deserve a whole book all on their own, but this phenomenon is so common it bears mentioning. Many querents want readings about their love interests, but it is when they use the word "soul mate" that raises red flags for me as a reader. Most of the time, querents are using the term to signify a particularly intense bond with someone else. But usually what they are experiencing is called a trauma bond.

One hallmark of a trauma bond is having an explosive, intense beginning energy that becomes inconsistent after the initial period. The partner is only intermittently responsive to the needs of your querent, and it is the partner who decides when, how, and how often connection between them happens. Your querent cannot rely on their partner but because of the intensity of the bond, has a very hard time walking away. There is often an addiction element to relationships like this due to its very inconsistent nature.

A trauma bond causes incredible anxiety and insecurity for a querent, and it is in this state they seek a reading, usually as reassurance that the soul mate will begin to act right and their lives together can begin afresh. However, your reading will no doubt offer a very different message. Move forward carefully, because depending on where your querent is in the process, they will either see the message as a sobering pail of refreshing cold water, or as an attack on their dream.

If you get the sense that your querent may be in a trauma bond you can ask them something like, "Are you okay with moving forward on this reading if there is a possibility that it tells you the relationship has no future?" If they respond with an emotional tone to your question or are even visibly shaking, they may not be ready. Offer to read for them another day.

If the querent decides to move forward, continue to communicate clearly and faithfully. Read what you see, but do not take on their emotions. They may be relieved, afraid, angry, or sad—most of the time, these emotions will be loud. A reading that tells them they cannot have their "soul mate" is like telling an addict they cannot have their drug of choice. They may respond irrationally to you or the reading. If they become disrespectful or even belligerent, end the session.

In all cases, I would refer the querent to a therapist; trauma bonding results from a complex map of factors that may include C-PTSD, attachment issues, and family abuse. These querents typically need significant support to help them shake off a "soul mate."

Querents Who Say the Reading Is Totally Wrong (But You Sense It Is Right)

- "How could a woman cause trouble at work? I only work with men and we get along really well!"
- "What do you mean a layoff is imminent?! Everything is fine!"

- "My sister is my best friend; she would never share my secret."
- "My husband will never find out. It's impossible."

It is such a challenge when your cards are flowing with a message that is clear as day but your querent shakes their head and tells you that everything you are saying is wrong. It can really throw us off if we are not prepared.

Querents tend to have what I call a "radius of plausibility," which means that they have an unconscious guess as to what the reading will cover. If it is outside of what they think is plausible, they will reject the information. And although rejection like this is often a sign that the message was outside of the querent's radius of plausibility, it does not mean it is wrong.

People often express rejection when they are surprised. Think about it this way. If someone was told that their dog was run over, they will respond with rejection: "That can't be. I left him inside!" People will also reject good news like winning the lottery: "No way! Me? Are you sure? Check the numbers again!" It doesn't matter if the information is perceived as good or bad. Resistance and rejection happen if a person sees the message as implausible.

When a querent rejects information, I recommend staying loyal to the message. If the reading rings true for you, you have to stick to your "divinatory guns," despite how they react. "I know this sounds surprising. Can you just keep it in mind as a data point? If it's wrong, it's wrong, but we may not know that yet."

One of the frustrating things about being a reader is that we often bear the brunt of someone's immediate, negative reaction. It could be years later before you learn that the reading was indeed right. Don't let these interactions fluster you; you aren't writing the message, you are just delivering it.

Querents Who Say They Already Knew What You Told Them (and Not in a Good Way)

It takes far more skill for a reader to confirm what is known than it is to read about something that may or may not happen five years from now. A reader telling the querent that she is having problems with her boss and that her son recently got in trouble at school are both things the querent can immediately verify. This is the mark of a great reader!

Readings about our common lives may not be as exciting or woo-woo as readings about past lives, the future ten years from now, or news that a querent has an intergenerational curse on them. And yet, these readings cannot be immediately verified as true by the querent. So why would some querents dismiss the former and give credibility to the latter? Querent reader style mismatch.

When a querent says something like, "You didn't tell me anything I didn't already know," it often indicates an expectation of a reading that follows a certain style of reader, the kind who are more interested in straight prediction or woo-woo topics than working on current events. The querent wants you to tell her that she will win the lottery in five years, and that her daughter will give her three beautiful grandbabies. She wants to peek into the mystery, she wants to know about her past life, or that her favorite aunt is visiting from the other side. She wants an hour where she gets to be immersed in something mystical, special, and different. The last thing she wants is to talk about her same old life; why the hell do that?

The thing is, there is nothing wrong with her expectations at all. But if you are coming to her with, "Let's look at what is going on now in your life and see how we can navigate it" or "Let's unpack that traumatic situation," she won't be interested, and that is okay.

The problem is that most people think that all tarot readers are the same and that tarot is used in the same way. So either the querent did not listen to your spiel in the beginning which should briefly explain your approach, or you did not tell her. She assumed you would be like other readers, so when you gave her something different, she was disappointed.

The other possible problem is that you as the reader did not listen to her to see if you could offer her what she wanted. If you plowed ahead thinking that what you had to offer her was better, then you let your own sense of righteousness get in the way of two key pieces: communication and consent. The solution is easy: give her your spiel at the start of the session. Ask for questions so you understand where her expectations lie, and if you cannot deliver, offer alternatives with her consent or let her go.

Querents Who Are Disappointed in the Direction the Reading Went

This is a challenge I see specifically among newer readers, and it can be an issue around inexperience. Some beginning readers forget that the reading is usually answering the question. When they look at the cards, they see another narrative that is easier to write, so they may riff on that. But in most cases, the cards are answering the question. If we find ourselves going down a rabbit hole, we have to check ourselves. Are we saying this because it is answering the question, or because it's easier to read the cards this way?

If we communicate, ask for questions, and approach the session from a querent-led philosophy, it will be rare for a querent to feel as though the direction went somewhere they did not also want to go in. Sometimes we do experience that "tarot override" effect where tarot has other plans about what it wants to talk about, but we should still ask for consent to proceed.

The Reading Cannot Call a Prediction

Every once in a while, a reading just cannot call the prediction. Even when you try to get at the question from another angle, you just get that "Ask again later" vibe. As maddening as it can be, it does happen, and often for good reason. Sometimes the reason is that the prediction is so close to going either way that the reading cannot call it just yet. There are too many factors in flux, and the confidence in the prediction either way is low. I see this often in situations where a querent has interviewed for a position and the person involved in making the decision keeps vacillating between the querent and another applicant. Once again, we have to be loyal to the message. As much as it may pain our querent to hear, we cannot determine the prediction— we just cannot.

Reader's Tip

Offer to give the reading a few days and try again. Sometimes the things in flux will have moved enough to shift the prediction one way or another.

Querents Who Want a Reading on the Same Question Repeatedly

Repeated requests to read on the same thing is typically about the desire to ease anxiety (and is totally normal too). When I was house hunting, I asked the cards the same question so many times that I swear I thought my deck was going to walk out on me. When a prediction is taking longer than we think it should, we start to worry. And when we worry, we seek reassurance.

Unless something major that could affect the outcome has shifted or there is a new variable in play, however, I try not to repeat the same question too close to the previous reading. I want to see how the prediction will unfold as we saw it. We either trust our prediction or don't. And if we don't, why are we asking in the first place?

Tell your querent that another reading too soon on the same question may give them the opposite effect. Instead of rereading the same question, ask your querent if there is another question that you two can do together that will ease her worries. Perhaps she needs confirmation that she has made the right decision or needs to check in with why it might be taking longer than the first reading indicated.

Reader's Tip

Just because sessions should be querent-led doesn't mean you are required to answer their questions. If you feel that the repeated request for the same question is stemming from an unhealthy place or your own frustration is getting in the way, refuse to conduct the reading. You don't have to just because they want you to!

Querents Directing Their Anger at the Reading Toward You

People often transfer their anger at systems or power toward the frontline people where they can direct their fury. They also might be transferring how they feel about someone (their anger at an ex-lover that the reading was about) onto you. Sometimes they might even challenge the reading and try to argue with you.

If the querent is being belligerent and disrespectful, end the session immediately. No one has time for that nonsense. If the querent isn't necessarily disrespectful but their anger is interfering with your ability to read, call out the behavior. "Hey, don't shoot the messenger!" or "You are welcome to be as mad at the tarot cards as you want. Tarot can take it. I, on the other hand, cannot."

There are times where you may be forced to be confrontational in order to preserve your boundaries. If you need to immediately stop the session, turn your cards down and fold your hands in your lap. Calmly say, "I cannot read with the energies present at this time. It appears that I am not the reader for you, so let's call it a day." Most people are shocked when you reaffirm boundaries peacefully. Whatever the querent does, stay calm and continue to repeat yourself as you stand up and walk to the door. If you are online, end the call.

Querents Expecting a Reading to Cover All Questions

Don't rush to try to fit in everything the querent wants in a reading, even if it means that they have some unanswered questions when your time is up. If you two agreed on a set time together and you've got to go, you've got to go! This does not mean that the querent gets to railroad those last two questions into the last five minutes of the session.

The length of a reading is just the amount of time you have agreed to read for them; it is not a guarantee on what you can cover within that time frame. Readings tend to unfold as they need to, not as the querent wants them to. As a reader for others, do your best but don't let anyone bully you into producing an inferior reading because they want everything before time's up. Quality is always better than quantity when it comes to most things in life, including readings.

Querents Pushing for More Time

Some querents will push you for more time no matter what. They will always have one more question, so can you please answer one more? It's not just you—these types of people are always trying to get more. Asking for an extra-large scoop of ice cream at the shop, asking the cashier to apply another coupon on top of their other five, expecting the hair stylist to throw in a glaze for free. These people are entitled and have also learned that pushing often gets them what they want.

Do not, I repeat, do not indulge in pushing behavior. Please trust me on this: pushy people are not testing you to see how nice of a person you are. They are testing you to see what they can get away with. Indulging them doesn't mean they see you as nice—it means they see you as a mark. Once they see that you are an easy mark, they will start testing your boundaries in other ways. You say "okay, five more minutes," and the next thing you know they're blowing up your phone at 3 o'clock in the morning demanding another reading.

You are probably thinking, "What does one extra question actually hurt, Jenna?" but here's the thing: everything that is sustainable has boundaries. You have to pick up your kid from daycare at a set time. Her dance class is exactly forty minutes. You go to sleep at midnight—everything has a beginning, middle, and end. A reading is no different. It shouldn't just keep going and going until the querent feels like ending it.

Reader's Tip

Your boundaries protect you. Having boundaries does not mean you are a bad person or a bad reader. Having boundaries does not mean that you are less spiritual.

Querents Who Return to Say the Reading Was Wrong

Readings can be wrong. We can be wrong. There are so many reasons why a prediction can go wrong. As readers, we want to be curious (not avoidant) if a querent tells us that a prediction was wrong. It's also possible that the reading was right but the querent understood it differently or remembered incorrectly; there are so many factors in play.

If the querent is open to it, I will do another reading asking what happened. Often this will give me the information I need. I also review my notes to see if there was something I missed in the reading. I also manage querent expectations from the beginning of the session by stating clearly that a prediction is just that: a prediction—not a guarantee.

Have we fired all meteorologists for giving inaccurate forecasts? Have we pushed all investment account fund managers into the sea for buying the wrong index funds before a crash? If the answer is no, then why turn away tarot as a predictive tool because it gets things wrong sometimes?

Querents Who Ask, "Why Did Tarot Tell Me Something Completely Different a Year Ago?"

Here is a nearly real-life example from a querent. "Last year when we did a reading, the tarot said I should take this job. At the time I was not sure if I wanted to take it, but I also needed a job. However, I am still unhappy. But now the reading is indicating that I should leave. Why would a reading tell me to take a job and then leave it? Isn't that conflicting advice?"

The question is simple enough but the answer is complex. Recalling chapter 5, "If You're the Reader, Who Is the Writer?," we remember that tarot is a probability crunching machine that considers all possible outcomes and chooses only one to share. The one it shares is the one it has determined to be in the querent's greatest good at that moment based on the factors in play at the time. Therefore, it is a mistake to assume that the path taken meant that the advice was wrong or wasted just because the advice is different at a later time.

Instead of panicking because a querent is calling you to account, what you can do is pull apart the scenario and do hypothetical readings. For example, we can do a reading on, "What would have happened if the querent did not take this job at that time?" Remember the "almost pasts" from chapter 5? They really come in handy here. We can also ask something like, "Did taking this job at this time position me for something better later on in a way that nothing else could?"

We can help our querents see predictions as suggestions on a near-future path rather than one right answer for the future for all time. This more flexible understanding of tarot (and the future) fosters a greater capacity for flexibility and resilience. It makes room for an expanding universe and an extraordinary life.

Querents Who Need to Be Fired

How do you fire a querent? It can be so tricky because if they are a friend or family member, it could cause a rift in the relationship. Normally, I try to go the subtle route: I will be suddenly unavailable, take a long time to respond to requests, or say that I am taking a break from doing readings.

If the subtle approach does not work, being direct is next. Directness is tough because people don't take kindly to rejection. There can be backlash, but ask yourself if the backlash is better or worse than how reading for them made you feel. A direct approach means ripping the bandage off, so to speak. State clearly to the person that you are unable to read for them anymore. You don't owe them any explanations. After that, refuse to engage in any further discussion on it. Usually it takes a special kind of person to even get to this point; it's likely this person has trodden all over your boundaries a bunch of times already. It should be clear to you that this person cannot really see beyond their needs and wants, so any reasons given to them will often be used as ammo against you. It's just not worth it.

I know it is always so hard to banish someone from your circle. Every time I have had to do this I was stressed. It took a long time in some circumstances before I pulled the trigger and just did it. But I can also tell you that letting people go from my life who were taking rather than adding to it only made my life better in the long run.

You don't owe anyone a reading, but you do owe it to yourself to ensure that people are coming to you correctly. Stand with strength and give harmful people the boot.

Over-relying on Querent Feedback as an Indicator of Your Success

You cannot always gauge your effectiveness as a reader from querent feedback alone. By the very emotional and transactional nature of a reading, a querent may not be the best person to play arbiter of your reading success; they are only able to provide feedback from their point of view. If you gave them a reading with information they disliked, for example, they might equate that with you giving them a bad reading when the reading was actually quite good. Relying only on querent feedback as a source for determining whether you are a good reader or not is a mistake. You need other ways to see how you are doing, such as recordings of your readings to identify what was done well and what needs work. Alternatively, create a reader's circle where other readers can give each other feedback in reader, querent, and observer roles. You will learn a lot this way.

Activity
From Fear to Fortitude—
A Powerful Tarot Technique to
Conquer Anxiety and Build Resilience

Our best readings come from a place centered on our querents and the reading. But when a reading goes south, it can shake our confidence to the core. Unresolved insecurity works against a reading, and as our anxiety asserts itself, if wants to take center stage. It no longer lets us center the reading on the querent and the message. Finding ways to process moments that fuel insecurity not only heals our wounds but also makes us better readers for others. Difficult sessions are lessons wrapped as opportunities to be better readers. With the right tools, we become readers who have confidence, good boundaries, and resilience.

Here is one tool that can help you on this journey toward greater fortitude. For this activity you need your deck, a writing implement, and a couple of pieces of paper. I think it is best to do this activity analog with real paper and pen.

Part One: Fear

Flip your deck faceup and choose an image that represents a time where you had a reading go bad. (If this has not happened for you yet, choose an image that best represents your inner fears as you consider beginning to read for others.) Pull that card out of the deck and prop it up so you can look at it easily. Let's call this the fear card.

Imagine the fear card as a symbol or archetype made real that can talk. For example, if you chose the Five of Swords, you might imagine that card as a bully taunting you or taking away something important of yours.

Next, take a piece of paper and draw a line down the middle. Ask the fear card what it thinks about you in regard to the bad situation on your mind. As it talks to you, write down everything it says without filtering or responding. Write everything down but only on the left side of the paper, leaving the right side clean.

Continuing the example, say that your Five of Swords fear card says something like, "You will never be strong enough to stand up for yourself." Write down what it says. Once you are done, read through everything. Truly look at what has been written there. Feel the emotions you need to feel as you look at these terrible words. If it gets too intense at any time, take a break and come back to it another time. Or choose a different fear card to work with for now.

Part Two: Guardian

Keep your fear card out of the deck for this next part. Take the rest of the deck and flip it facedown once again as you normally do and shuffle. As you shuffle, ask, "Who is my guardian right now?" Choose one card. If you get another difficult card (such as Death or the Ten of Swords), that is totally fine. Even tough cards can be your guardian.

Next, imagine the guardian card as a symbol or archetype made real that can talk. For example, if you drew the Queen of Swords, you might imagine that card as a powerfully intelligent woman speaking for you, standing in front of you and protecting you.

Next, take the papers on which you wrote what the fear card had to say. Ask your guardian to respond to the messages from your fear card but write those responses in the right-hand column. So, if the Five of Swords card wrote, "You will never be strong enough to stand up for yourself" on the left-hand side of the paper, the Queen of Swords might respond on the right side with something like, "She has everything within her to stand up to bullies like you. She is strong. She is intelligent. She is fair."

Once finished, read over the guardian's words. See the kind words and compassion your guardian brings to the table. See how silly or illogical much of the fear card's words were in the light of the guardian's truth. Allow yourself to feel supported and loved.

Part Three: Fortitude Magic

Look through the sentences channeled from your guardian. Choose three sentences that feel particularly meaningful and relevant. Once you've chosen your three sentences, rewrite them as factual "I" statements. For example, if your guardian said something like: "She is great at being kind and compassionate," rewrite it as an "I" statement. "I am a kind and compassionate reader."

Turning guardian statements into "I" statements helps to cognitively overwrite the neurological programming from "fear" statements to "power" statements. Basically, you are adding volume to the parts of you that believe in you, want the best for you, and see your gifts. And magically, you are manifesting this truth each time you speak them. You can use this mini spell anytime you start to feel insecure. You can also say it to yourself as a private act of energetic housekeeping before you begin reading for another.

Reading for others guarantees that you will have sessions that don't go well. Even if you have been reading for twenty years, bad readings happen, and that is okay—you are human! With your very own spell for fortitude when these things happen, you will be able to manage challenges more quickly without breaking your stride.

Extra Credit

Write a paragraph or two about your guardian using these questions as prompts:

★ Why do you think this particular guardian appeared?
★ What is the message, or truth, that this guardian is bringing to you?
★ Is this a card you normally see as a guardian? Why or why not?
★ Does the guardian represent someone in your life who protected or promoted you in the past? Is the guardian an aspect of you?

15

A Guide to Self-Care for Those Not Great at Self-Care

At first, reading tarot for someone is exhilarating. There is definitely a "reader's high," a rush that is honestly a bit addictive. Where does this euphoria come from? I think it comes from Spirit; while in our role as readers, we are connected to a live wire from the Universe. To help us do our work, we get a boost of power that comes with the information that we are relaying. And with that power boost, it is not uncommon for a reader to conduct readings for eight hours straight, forgetting to eat or take a break. It is only once the work is over that they realize their back is hurting, their throat is dry, and they can barely string two sentences together. Many often completely crash the next day, unable to get off the couch while wondering, "Why am I so tired?" They are surprised to see how much reading tarot can take out of them.

> **Reader's Tip**
> Reading stamina is a thing. With practice and healthy habits, however, your capability to read will grow before depleting you.

There are many reasons as to why readers experience fatigue; a lot goes on, more than just "reading cards." Here are some of the things you are doing while in a reading with someone:

- Gathering psychic impressions (if that is what you do)
- Navigating and grounding querent emotions (especially for empaths)
- Reading the cards and knitting them to impressions and the querent
- Listening to the querent to deeply understand what they need
- Tuning out ambient noise and distractions
- Watching for body language to see if there is something you need to clarify
- Asking thoughtful questions to ensure you are on the same page
- Wording your reading in ways that are sensitive and unique to that individual
- Shielding your own energy, interacting with theirs, having Universal energy flow through you as you guide it toward the reading
- Chatting with random spirits that show up (if you are mediumship-inclined)
- Doing all of this in a choreography so they get what they need within the time frame you have determined together

Wow! That's a lot of things, isn't it? No wonder this is a lot of work! You are like a shaman, a symbologist, a medium, an empath, a teacher, a counselor, an organizer, a facilitator, and a manager all rolled into one. If you were a computer, it would look like you have twenty tabs open all at once! But unlike a computer, we can't add another memory stick to our heads (at least not yet, anyway), so we have to take good care of what we've got so it lasts a long time.

Reader's Tip

Some people (okay, me) find it hard to practice self-care. Many of us learned somewhere along the way that working relentlessly while ignoring our own needs is the way to go. Some of us internalized the message that self-care is selfish and self-indulgent. That isn't the case at all. In fact, self-care is hard work, even when it looks easy. Taking care of ourselves increases our capacity to help others. Self-care is not only recommended, it is imperative.

The Things That Wear You Down

Repetitive Motion Injury

I know it might sound surprising, but reading tarot is quite a physical job. In the early years of reading, I developed tennis elbow (lateral epicondylitis). It took forever to figure out why, since I don't play tennis. Turns out it was a repetitive motion injury from shuffling.

Looks Versus Comfort

Many readers dream about their cool reading nook; perhaps it is Victorian-themed with a crushed velvet couch and a cute writing table illuminated by candlelight. Do that for too long, however, and your body will begin to complain. Your back will begin hurting from being scrunched up over the small table, and eye strain and fatigue from reading in poor light will cause headaches. I learned the hard way that what looks good and what works best don't always align. As my grandma used to say, "Choose shoes for your feet, not your head."

Dealing with Imposter Syndrome

One of the greatest ongoing challenges readers face is imposter syndrome. Even readers who have been at it for years will suddenly find themselves in thought patterns such as, "Why are people coming to me for advice? Do I really know what I am doing? Maybe I am just pretending. My own life is a mess, who am I to help another?" All of us have these thoughts at various times in our lives, and it's completely normal to have them. Thoughts like these are not a sign that you are an imposter—they are, in fact, a sign that you are *not*.

Bad Reading, Bad Querent

At some point in your tarot journey, you are going to have a bad reading. Even if you are doing all the right things, something will happen every once in a while that shakes your confidence to its core, perhaps so much so that you question whether you should continue to read for others. Once again this is normal, and it happens to most if not all readers. How we deal with bad readings is a critical factor because we can either give up or use these moments to build our capacity for resilience. You don't need to have unshakable faith in tarot or your readings, but what you do absolutely need, my friend, is an unshakable faith in yourself.

Boredom

Reading for people means getting the same questions over and over again. Maybe you find yourself stifling a yawn after one more, "How does he feel about me?" question. Don't ignore your boredom. Boredom is the "check engine light" that comes before burning out. If you find yourself "phoning it in" or saying the same things the same way and using the same sentences and idioms. Pay attention as you are in dangerous territory.

Compassion Fatigue

People in helping professions are the most susceptible to compassion fatigue. If you find yourself waiting for the reading to be over already, you have compassion fatigue. If you stop being curious, feel numb, or don't really care even though you know you should, you have compassion fatigue. If you are secretly rolling your eyes, find yourself becoming judgmental and even callous, these are all signs of compassion fatigue. The CHECK ENGINE warning that lit up when you were merely bored has now turned into smoke coming from under your hood. Take your foot off the gas and pull over now.

Burnout

The next stop on the train of ignoring self-care is burnout. The smoke coming from under your hood has turned into you broken down at the side of the road in the middle of nowhere with no cell service. Burnout as a reader means that you are exhausted. You have no more to give anyone. You don't want to read for anyone anymore, maybe ever. Burnout leads to physical problems that are stress-related. Burnout also affects your personal relationships. You may struggle with your moods and use substances such as food, alcohol, or drugs to cope. You may feel as though you have no control over your life. The spark has been blown out.

The insidious danger of burnout is that it resists resolution. Part of its pattern is making you cynical. And once cynicism sets in, it becomes much harder for interventions to take hold as you may be resistant to them. This is why I stress weekly emotional check-ins and taking care of yourself before getting to this point. This is not a place you ever want to find yourself in.

Do What Refills Your Mind, Body, and Soul

Now that I have sufficiently warned you about what it might look like if you are not taking care of yourself, here's a list of things that will help tremendously. You may also come up with your own solutions. Overall, the thing about the practice of self-care is that it is a practice. Thinking about the things you can do—but not doing them—won't work. You have to make the time. You have to create the space. You have to prioritize yourself.

Ergonomics

Ergonomics is your friend. You need a table at a comfortable height so you can sit upright and not be hunched over a coffee table trying to shuffle. You need a chair that actually supports your body. You need good lighting to see the cards. You need to be able to speak at a volume that won't blow your voice out. If you're in a space over which you don't have direct control (such as when doing party readings in someone's home or working from a New Age bookstore), advocate for yourself. Tell people what you need. Listen to your body.

Body Mechanics

Use proper posture and take care to avoid repetitive motion injuries. Not sure what proper posture looks like? Record yourself reading and take a look to see what your body is doing. Consciously correct your slouch and keep your feet on the floor. By the way, if you ever get tennis elbow, look up the Flex Bar. It is a device that allows you to build the muscles in your forearm and retrain your alignment.

Good Old-Fashioned Healthy Habits

We readers have a tendency to forget about the rest of us attached to our heads and hands. Add readings into the equation and that euphoria we get from doing them, and our poor bodies are low on the list of things we notice. Because of these aspects, we need to prioritize good body care such as eating well, moving our bodies, sleeping well, and breathing well, too. Now, you have heard me say earlier that living healthfully doesn't make you a better reader or psychic and that is true. But, living healthfully does make doing readings easier because you have the foundation you need to support the rest.

Journal

Journaling is your budget-friendly, ever nonjudgmental listening ear for you to get all of that stuff in your head, out. Even if you burn it after writing, it has done its job. The point of this journal is not to use it as a technique for replaying your sessions but rather as a place to help you process sessions so that your brain isn't waking you up at 3 o'clock in the morning with a rousing, "Ding-dong! Remember when you totally said the wrong thing?! Let's replay it right now!" Make sure that you find a safe place for your journaling, or burn it after reviewing it. It is for your eyes alone. Your querents place an incredible amount of trust in you, guard that trust faithfully.

Let Nature Heal

The well-established research around the healing power of nature cannot be overstated. We've known this for a long time. Most of our ancient sacred places were out in nature, and the people who made pilgrimages to them were healed both by the natural world and their spiritual practice. Do not underestimate the healing power of a long walk in the woods, the mountains, the desert, or the sea. Make time for this. While you are at it, put your phone on Do Not Disturb and have someone watch the kids.

Keep Things Fresh

Don't let yourself get too comfortable with a reading style or technique that you like. Keep pushing the boundaries of your tarot practice. Learn a new technique, a new divination style, or offer a unique twist on a reading. Teach a class. Nothing is as motivating as watching new people fall in love with tarot!

Find Something Unique

Have you ever been scared or hurt and a nurse, police officer, teacher, or some other authority figure has acted abrupt and distant? I bet it sucked, didn't it? I always think about the one time I went to the emergency room scared and hurting, only to find that the people around me acted like I wasn't even really there; they were so over it. I never want to be that person. I never want to stop seeing people, I mean really *seeing* them. That said, it is hard when we see the same thing repeatedly. We can become a bit numb.

One technique I use to combat that indifference is to find something unique about the querents. What is one thing about them that makes them special? Perhaps you can even incorporate that into the session. You can do readings asking about their unique gifts and strengths in addition to the usual questions. Find a way to get curious about every single person you read for. Remember that while you may have heard the question a million times already, it is most likely the first time for them.

Tarot Activities

One of the reasons why I included the kinds of activities in this book that I did was to give you a small tool kit that you can turn to when you are just not feeling up to it. These activities are not to be done just one time but are there for you whenever you need. You use tarot to help others so much, also remember to use tarot for yourself. Tarot heals you, too!

Reader's Tip

Build your own tarot resource binder full of spreads and activities that you find particularly helpful and meaningful. You can even arrange them by problem such as "anxiety" or "boredom." Then, when you are struggling, choose an activity that would best help with the area you are feeling challenged in.

Encourage Proactive Readings

Talk to your querents about getting proactive readings. Tell them not to wait until the you-know-what has hit the fan. For example, encourage them to get a reading on relationship dynamics in the beginning, or when first starting a new job. That way, the information will be far more helpful than information given in a reading when the querent is hanging on by a thread and looking for a miracle. The number one reason readers emotionally burn out is that it is exhausting to deal with one emotional emergency after another. We can help querents see a reading as an intervention rather than a Hail Mary, which means we get to do what we want tarot to do—help—rather than asking tarot for the impossible.

Psychological Support

As a reader, you are going to hear things from querents that you might not be able to shake. Often, querents are so fully in their own pain that they may not realize that what they are saying might be difficult for you to hear. Laypeople do not realize how much emotional labor our work requires, which makes your role similar to that of a therapist or social worker. And what therapists do when they need support is get therapy. Being able to debrief a session with a therapist can help you process what you heard in a healthy way.

Social Connections

I have a wonderful friendship with a few people in which we talk about everything except tarot. They never ask me for readings, and they don't even ask me questions about what it is like being a reader. Instead, we sing karaoke, laugh at dumb jokes, and play board games. With them, I am Jenna the person, not Jenna the reader. Friends like these are gold to me.

Because of the emotional labor I do as a reader, I need people and places where I will not be asked to play that role. It is hard because I have a natural tendency to play helper, and most readers do; we are healers by nature. Having friends who are just interested in what to bring over on board game night is a gift. Find these friends and treasure them. They will often have no idea how important they can become for you.

> ## Reader's Tip
> Be careful not to mistake the intimacy and vulnerability that comes with readings as real friendship. Querents *do* seem like friends—they care about you and ask you how you are. Readings *do* seem like two friends enjoying each other's company, but that relationship can be one-sided.

Over the years as a tarot reader, I've had a number of querents seek out friendship. I personally prefer professional distance, so when this happens, I give them a choice: stay as my querent or become my friend but you can't be both. There were times when I attempted to let querents become friends, but often they could not stop seeing me as their reader. Even in friendship we still had a dynamic of me playing helper, which created a lopsided friendship. I have only one successful exception to this rule after many attempts.

Have Fun

Most of the time, readings can be intense and serious work. Finding a hobby that is just pure fun is powerful prevention against compassion fatigue. One thing I did was to take an improv class. Spending an hour laughing your head off and acting silly can be a wonderful healing practice. If improv isn't your thing, make sure that whatever you do includes a sense of play. I recommend finding something that has no other purpose than bringing you joy. If that activity is tied to another agenda, it doesn't count. Intentionally find ways to "waste time" in pleasant ways.

Take a Break

Maybe the break is just a week or a month, but for some readers it can be years. There is no right or wrong way to decide how much time you need. When I sense I am not able to muster curiosity or if I am flagging in my compassion, I take a break. What works for me is a week off every ten weeks or so; sometimes I need a month off too. I know when I am ready to return when I find myself missing reading tarot again. If I find my hands itching to read cards for someone, I know it's go time.

Activity
Practice Self-Care

Take a break. You need it and, more importantly, you deserve it.

16
Ready for the Woo?

This chapter is a collection of interesting experiences I've encountered as a reader for others. Some of what I say may land for you, and some of it might sound totally out in the land of the woo. Readers have a wide variety of belief systems, so please take what feels apt and leave the rest.

The Mundane Is Divine

I've come to realize that seemingly random things that happen during a session may not be so random after all. The phone chiming, an ambulance wailing past, a car with a song playing—pay attention to what was being said in the reading when this happens. This is often an event that acts to reinforce the message. When this happens, bring your querent's attention to it.

Their Ears Are Burning

This is a very common phenomenon: a querent is talking about someone and guess what? That person has just texted them or is calling. I've seen it happen even if the other person is not particularly close to the querent but we were either talking about them or the reading included them in some way. I think what is happening is that the other person is sensing the reading's focus on them. Generally, they don't even know why they felt compelled to call.

Additionally, I find that if I am thinking about someone, within days they'll reach out to get a reading with me. Am I sensing them? Are they sensing me? Who knows! Either way, this happens very often in reader-querent relationships and deserves a mention.

Coincidence and Synchronicity

It is quite common for my querents to book readings a year later to the day of the previous reading, usually with no idea that they were so unconsciously accurate! I've also read for querents with the same exact birth date or first name who get readings all on the same day. It is very common to get nothing but Capricorns one week and Leos the next.

It is also common to have stalker cards that keep showing up again and again, or it can seem as though the same message keeps popping up through a series of querents. Sometimes these runs mean that the Universe is trying to send you, the reader, a message. If you notice these coincidences and synchronicities, do a reading for yourself to determine if the Universe is trying to get your attention.

Deck Vibes

Sometimes a deck that used to work like a charm now seems totally off, or you may find that the deck is reading in a particularly darker way than usual. You may also get the sense that the deck reads off when being used in a certain way or with certain people.

Some of my decks only work for me and no one else. Other decks were not a match for my energy and I had to give them away. What is going on here? I don't know, exactly. Perhaps I am just anthropomorphizing my decks and projecting things onto them. Maybe there is an energy imprint left from the creators. Maybe querents are putting their own anxious vibes on the deck. Whatever the case may be, I listen to my decks; if they aren't working for me, I try to fix it. This could mean putting them away for a while, giving them away to someone else, only using them in certain situations, or clearing the bad vibe.

One other phenomenon I've noticed but cannot explain is that a deck that reads well may not look the part. Decks that I love visually don't always work well for doing readings. I also have decks that aren't my visual cup of tea but read great! It is an annoying side effect that is expensive to find out for yourself!

Some People Are Easier to Read Than Others

Why do you nail a reading on one day but not on another? Controlling for all factors, why is one querent's boyfriend easy to read about but another's feels like you are trying to see through mud? The reasons may not have anything to do with you but instead the energy the other person is bringing to the table. Here are some of the most common aspects of this phenomenon in readings.

If someone is psychic, it is relatively easier for me to read for them, as though their signal is loud and clear. Just noticing how easy or hard it is for me to pick up impressions tells me about the querent's psychic talents. If you find this is also true for you, this might be why.

The way I pick up psychic information resembles links on a chain: the querent is the first link, my contact. It is then through the querent I pick up subsequent links (people) connected to them. For example, say a querent wants a reading about her young adult son. No problem, mothers to their children are incredibly easy. Those links sing. But if she wanted me to read about her son and his new girlfriend, it becomes harder. If she wanted to know about her son's girlfriend's boss, it is even harder still. I have to link querent to son to girlfriend to boss, and the more links I am jumping, the more those impressions degrade. This may be unique to the way I pick up impressions; your mileage may vary. But if this makes sense to you, rock on.

Ease of reading variability is also affected by how close the querent is to someone that they wish the reading to include. If I can easily pick up the third person, it typically means that they are close with the querent. If I have to work at picking up the third person, it indicates to me that they are distant.

If someone wants me to read about them and a new love interest and the impressions of the other person are clear, it often indicates that they are both wanting to be in a relationship with each other. But if that love interest is hard to pick up and the details are fuzzy, that can often mean that they might not be as interested as the querent.

Skeptics and other closed-off people are harder still. The "prove it to me" energy is so aggressive and closed, it feels like I'm being asked to sculpt a clay bowl while wearing boxing gloves. I hate this kind of attitude because the skeptic already has a confirmation bias (to debunk me) and comes in totally closed off to the point where I cannot sense anything, only confirming to them that they were right all along. I think why it bothers me so much is that we readers are unfairly made responsible for things not in our control. It is like ordering a meal, dumping the saltshaker on it, and then complaining that the dinner is terrible. Energetically, that is how it feels to me.

Interrupting Forces

As I typically have good control over my intuition, I rarely pick things up unless I go looking for them. But every once in a while, I am interrupted by someone or something that, in my mind's eye, appears as an image that comes out of nowhere. Unlike my usual impressions, these come with a very real sense of presence and always have a push and personality to them. These interrupters can be a wide range of things. Some are people who have crossed over and insist that I tell the querent something, some are angels, animals, guides, and even beings I can best describe as "interdimensional."

While noticing these presences occasionally feel eerie, I've never felt unsafe. Usually there is a feeling of intent to communicate or encourage, and, often, curiosity. No matter what I get, I always mention it no matter how weird it is. In fact, I remember one time looking at a querent and blurting out, "There is a raccoon next to you!" She smiled and said, "Well, that makes sense. Racoons are my favorite animal."

I work hard not to apply my own cosmology on anything I sense or see; that is not my role. I also don't try to judge what comes through. I am just passing along a message to the best of my ability, and sometimes those messages show up in interesting ways. If you get an interrupting force like this in a reading, I recommend dropping the reading as planned and allowing that entity to communicate (with querent's consent, of course)—it may have something incredibly important to say.

Psychic Vampires

Do you ever feel totally exhausted after just one reading? Does your head or stomach hurt after a session with someone? Pay attention to physical ailments because they can be a key indication of a psychic vampire. While the terminology is certainly hyperbolic, psychic vampires are usually strong empaths. So strong are they, in fact, that not only do they pull in your emotions, they pull in your energy, too. Most of the time, these people have no idea what they are doing. Either stop reading for them or do work to build incredibly strong energetic boundaries.

Psychic Emitters

Have you ever done a reading and afterward felt irrationally angry? How about happiness that comes from nowhere? You might have met an emitter. While empaths will pull from and reflect the emotions of others, these folks have an ability to make others feel what they are feeling. Emitters tend to have incredible charisma and are able to change the emotions and energy of a room. Like psychic vampires, many emitters have no idea they are affecting people. They might simply say that they have a way with people.

Emitter-type querents are actually harder for us to handle as readers because unlike the psychic vampires who are only pulling from us, emitters are making us feel things that could influence the reading. If the querent is an emitter who wants a specific outcome from the reading, the energy will be even more intense. Proceed only if you have strong shields.

Evil Eye

When someone is envious of someone else, it is like they are throwing darts of negativity at that person. Some people are naturally more capable of throwing these poisonous darts than others. It may be accidental, but it can also be quite intentional. You may suspect that someone is intentionally throwing the evil eye when it seems like you have an unusual string of bad luck after seeing someone. This issue can usually be turned around if you sense what is going on (more on that later in this chapter, under "Active Negative Energy Removal").

Passive Energy

Passive energy refers to the latent energetic atmosphere. It is not directed at anyone but affects people nevertheless. Here are two examples of passive energy to illustrate what I mean.

Recently, I went to see my hairdresser. Her salon is at the entrance to a mall; there are other shops nearby. Walking into the salon, I immediately felt something was off. The energy was subdued and anxious. It was so loud to me that I asked her if something happened. She told me that a week prior, there was a fight that broke out at the restaurant next door and guns were pulled. The combatants left the restaurant and chased each other in the mall with guns drawn. My stylist had to run to the back of the shop, and thankfully no one was hurt. Something happened in the space which left a kind of residue that affects everyone.

Similarly, ghostly hauntings can be the result of passive energy. People sometimes think they have an active poltergeist when they are actually dealing with a shell, a decaying energy pattern left by someone who crossed over. Shells usually dissipate on their own, but sometimes they stick around. The shell is like an old video stuck on repeat; there is no consciousness there. So if you are in the living room yelling, "Go toward the light, my friend!" and it doesn't work, this may be why. Tips for clearing this energy appears later in this chapter.

Active Energy

This is energy being consciously sent from one place to another. If you think of passive energy like the smell of perfume lingering in the air, think of active energy as the wind itself. It is on the move, and it may be directed to move toward you. The evil eye phenomenon above is one example of active energy: it has direction, movement, and a target.

As readers, we deal with energy all the time; sometimes it can be problematic for us. If energy is causing us a problem, we can learn to take care of it. But how we deal with passive versus active energy differs, and we shouldn't use the same tool for every problem. We need to use the right tool in the right way to make it work, and we need a game plan.

How to Manage Problematic Passive Energy

With passive energy, the space needs to be cleared, like a good dusting. Next, heal anything that was damaged due to that negative energy sitting around and causing problems. The space should then be protected so that the energy remains healthy and attracts positivity to the space.

If you do the clearing but not the replacement, you are just allowing negative energy a chance to reassert itself. If you've ever heard someone say something like, "I am saging this place like crazy, but it isn't working," it is likely because they are clearing but not protecting and attracting good energy. Since nature (and magic) hates a vacuum, we have to fill the vacuum we just created by introducing things that will make positive energy grow. All in all, passive energy removal is fairly straightforward, in three steps:

Passive Negative Energy Removal

Step 1. Clear passive negative energy

Step 2. Heal any damage done by passive negative energy

Step 3. Protect space and attract positivity

Active Negative Energy Removal

Active negative energy requires a different game plan. There are a few more steps, and it requires more effort. Like passive energy fixes that don't work, waving around some sage and tucking a black tourmaline in your bra isn't enough. Here are the steps for managing this mischief:

Choose 1a, 1b, or a combination of both.

Step 1a. Reverse the energy, like bouncing a ball back.

   OR

Step 1b. Dispel the charge, like dissipating a drop of wine in water.

Step 2. Shield by encircling your person or space so nothing can get in. (Some may disagree with me on this step and would prefer to clear first and then shield. But how can I sweep my house if the wind can still blow more dust in through the door?) You can also leave an "exhaust port" in your shields, allowing for anything remaining to find its way out as you do the clearing.

Step 3. Clear the space.

Step 4. Heal. (Check for damage. Has anything happened that needs repair? Does anything need energetic reinforcement?)

Step 5. Protect yourself and space. Maintain the space you just worked so hard to create.

Final Thoughts

Reading for others requires a tremendous amount of physical, mental, and energetic stamina. When we put ourselves first, we have better health outcomes. When we have better health outcomes, our capacity to help others increases.

If we are going to serve as messengers who remind others of their own innate worth, we must take the same advice, lest it ring hollow. We have to practice what we preach. We need to take care of ourselves without guilt or shame and treat ourselves as kindly as we treat our querents.

Activity
Build-A-Bewitchment

At the end of this chapter are lists of items, symbols, and interventions under each of these headings:

★ Clearing
★ Attracting or Emitting Positivity
★ Reversing the Charge
★ Defusing the Charge
★ Shielding
★ Healing

Like at "Build-A-Bear" shops, you are going to DIY your own energetic protections based on the formulas given for passive and active negative energy.

For practice, which formula would work best for each situation?

★ Your tarot deck is only giving negative readings.
★ You saw a querent and you felt exhausted after.
★ You notice your readings aren't as good whenever you read at a certain place.
★ A friend also reads tarot, but she never has anything nice to say about you. Since she started hanging out more you have noticed that strange things occur like getting a flat tire or picking up every cold that is going around.

Build-A-Bewitchment Resource List

The following list of items is by no means exhaustive; please consider it a jumping-off point for your own journey. Some items and activities will call to you, others will not. Feel free to come up with your own items and activities. You can also use something from a recommended list for another purpose. What is important is *your* visualization, *your* focus, and *your* belief that it will work. With visualization, focus, and belief in play, whatever feels most effective to you will be the most effective.

Reversing: Sending the Energy Back to Where It Came From

Items that will reverse negative energy when placed in strategic locations or worn:

★ Ba Gua mirror
★ Hand of Fatima or Hamsa
★ Hand with horned sign
★ Cowrie shell bracelets blessed by an elder
★ Nazar
★ Hex signs
★ Jet bracelet
★ Blue items
★ God's Eye
★ Upright horseshoe nailed over front door

Tarot cards that can be placed or worked with to reverse energy:

★ The Magician
★ The Moon
★ The Wheel of Fortune

Things to do when you sense active negative energy being directed at you:
★ Pinch yourself
★ Spit on the ground
★ Rub a pulled-out splinter in your hair (my grandma taught me this one)

★ Knock on wood
★ Tug an earlobe

Dispelling: Dissipating or Dispersing the Energy Rather Than Sending It Back

Passive things that will dispel energy:

★ Wind chimes
★ Open windows that allow a cross breeze
★ Pollinator gardens

Active things done to dispel energy:

★ Clapping
★ Cutting cords
★ Grounding negative energy into the earth
★ Throwing an ax into the ground

Powerful allies to invoke to assist in dispelling energy:

★ Archangel Gabriel
★ Snake, Butterfly, Lizard, Earthworm, Dandelion clans

Stones that can dispel energy when placed and worn:

★ Black obsidian
★ Tourmaline
★ Amber

Tarot cards that can be placed or worked with to dispel energy:

★ Temperance
★ Judgement
★ The Hanged Man
★ Death
★ The Tower

Shielding: Creating a Barrier Against Negative Energy

Things that can be placed or worn to shield the space or person:

★ Mezuzah
★ Black candle
★ Pentagram

- ★ Solomon's Seal
- ★ Broom leaning up against the door
- ★ Rosemary planted near the front door

Powerful allies to invoke to assist in shielding:

- ★ Archangel Michael
- ★ Turtle, Rhinoceros, Crab Rock clans

Stones when placed or worn to support the shield:

- ★ Black tourmaline
- ★ Black spinel
- ★ Chalcedony
- ★ Fire agate
- ★ Jasper
- ★ Obsidian
- ★ Onyx
- ★ Smoky quartz

Tarot cards that can be placed or worked with to support the shield:

- ★ The Emperor
- ★ The Hierophant
- ★ The Hermit

Things to do to shield your own energy:

- ★ Visualize a bubble or egg of white light surrounding you and your aura
- ★ Recite the last three surahs of the Quran
- ★ Recite the Lord's Prayer
- ★ Make the sign of the pentagram in all four directions with your dominant index finger

Clearing: Cleansing the Space or Yourself after You Have Put Protections in Place

Visualize a small, one-way port so the energy you are clearing can escape. Once finished, seal that port.

Things to do to clear the space:

- ★ Physically clean and declutter yourself and your space
- ★ Symbolically sweep the area or person with broom or peacock feather: up, down, counter-clockwise
- ★ Sprinkle charged water like Florida Water
- ★ Sprinkle salt in corners of the space or take a shower with a salt scrub

Items that can be used to clear the air:

- ★ Bells
- ★ Drums
- ★ Rattles
- ★ Tuning forks

Stones when placed or worn that aid in clearing people and places:

- ★ Selenite wands
- ★ Black kyanite
- ★ Copper
- ★ Brown jasper
- ★ Malachite

Clear the air with any of these:

- ★ White sage
- ★ Cedar
- ★ Copal
- ★ Frankincense
- ★ Juniper
- ★ Benzoin
- ★ Hyssop

Healing: Working to Repair Any Damage Resulting from Negative Energy in and around You

Things to do to heal:

- ★ Fix what's broken in the space or within you
- ★ Speak affirmations, such as "I am a whole person," or "I have everything I need"

- ★ Sing
- ★ Use Tibetan singing bowls
- ★ Light candles in green or white colors
- ★ Use Bach Flower Essences Rescue Remedy
- ★ Drink herbal infusions

Invoke Allies to Support Your Healing:

- ★ Archangel Raphael
- ★ Willow, Stream, Ocean, Soil, Songbird slans
- ★ Goddess Oya

Stones when worn or placed that facilitate healing:

- ★ Citrine
- ★ Agate
- ★ Bloodstone
- ★ Jade
- ★ Rose quartz
- ★ Carnelian
- ★ Star sapphire
- ★ Turquoise
- ★ Ametrine

Tarot cards that can promote healing when placed or worked with:

- ★ Temperance
- ★ The Star
- ★ The Empress
- ★ The Sun

Herbs and plants that promote healing when ingested, burned, infused, or grown:

- ★ Allspice
- ★ Angelica
- ★ Apple
- ★ Lemon balm
- ★ Peppermint

Protecting: Safeguarding the Hard Work You Have Done So That the Energy Remains Beneficial

There are two ways to do this: work on active protection (think security) and also promote beneficial energy to grow so negative energy has a harder time finding a spot to take hold.

Invite blessings from Allies such as:

- ★ Your ancestors
- ★ Divine light
- ★ Archangel Zadkiel
- ★ Devas and other spirits of place
- ★ Unicorn, Bear, Wolf, Thunder clans
- ★ Goddess Sekhmet
- ★ God Thor

Stones that facilitate protection when worn or placed:

- ★ Black tourmaline
- ★ Amber
- ★ Smoky quartz
- ★ Tiger's eye

Tarot cards that can protect when placed or worked with:

- ★ The Sun
- ★ The Magician
- ★ Strength
- ★ The Chariot

Herbs and Plants that can support protection:

- ★ Tea Tree
- ★ Anise
- ★ Bay
- ★ Clover
- ★ Fennel
- ★ Garlic
- ★ Mistletoe
- ★ Oak

Surround the space with things that generate positive energy:

★ Things that make you happy or remind you of a time you were happy such as family photos, mementoes, and children's art
★ Pets and houseplants for living energy
★ Invite good friends and hold celebrations; cultivate laughter
★ Reduce screen time and replace it with community time
★ Keep an altar with food and drink to make the devas happy
★ Sun-catchers
★ Water fountains
★ Pyramids

Herbs to promote positive energy:

★ Catnip
★ Hyacinth
★ Lavender
★ Meadowsweet
★ St. John's wort

Final Thoughts

It's a funny irony that we use tarot to find clarity in our lives but the exact manner in which tarot works is a mystery. Reading tarot well for others often requires one foot in the logical world and the other in the mystical, while also somehow being okay when those two worlds contradict one another. As readers, we are not obliged to make it all make sense. Rather, we find the sweet spot between revealing as much as we can while honoring the mystery.

My final piece of advice to you is to please keep a loose grip. Hold on to a thing, but not too tightly. Honor a belief, but change it if it no longer fits. Command respect, but also learn to laugh at your mistakes. Be responsible for your actions, but love yourself when those actions are less than ideal. We are all only human, after all.

May your tarot practice bring you laughter, humility, wisdom, and compassion. May reading tarot for others bring you meaning, healing, and peace. Finally, may tarot pull back the curtain and, with a wink, show you just enough because that's you—you are just enough, too.

Acknowledgments

To Barbara Moore and Llewellyn: thank you for seeing the potential in my proposal and deciding to work with me. To my beta readers, Lauren Lowe, Peg Cheng, Michael King, and Jennifer Mullenix: your insights and guidance made this a stronger book, many thanks. To the greater tarot community: you have inspired me, guided me, and lit the spark of oracle within me. It is on the shoulders of your work that I reach for the stars.

To the folks instrumental in supporting me through the process of writing my book: Nancy Antenucci, Melissa Cynova, Jaymi Elford, Kristine Gorman, Theresa Reed, Arwen Lynch Poe, Jamie Sawyer, and Benebell Wen: the emergency calls when I needed them, the texts, and DMs to keep me going. I admire you. I adore you. Thank you. To Rachel Pollack: for your prescient letters and for being a fellow time nerd. I treasure you.

To my clients, students, and mentees: you have given me more than I could have ever given you. Your stories, your lives, and your bright spirits have taught me so much. It has been an honor to work with you.

The years have been immeasurably kind to me in that I always had a family who believed me and believed *in* me; thank you. It is my incredible pleasure to be the "weird aunt," and I hope to give that title to whichever weird kid one of you has who knows more than she should.

Finally, to Rix: for the lessons in faith, hope, and loyalty. And of course, love.

Recommended Reading

Tarot

Books that are geared toward the reader-to-querent experience:

Antenucci, Nancy, and Melanie Howard. *Psychic Tarot: Using Your Natural Psychic Abilities to Read the Cards*. Woodbury, MN: Llewellyn Publications, 2012.

Ben Dov, Yoav. *The Marseille Tarot Revealed: A Complete Guide to Symbolism, Meanings & Methods*. Woodbury, MN: Lewellyn, 2017.

Cynova, Melissa. *Tarot Elements: Five Readings to Reset Your Life*. Woodbury, MN: Llewellyn Publications, 2019.

Fairfield, Gail. *Everyday Tarot: Using the Cards to Make Better Life Decisions*. Boston: Weiser, 2002.

Greer, Mary. *21 Ways to Read a Tarot Card*. St. Paul, MN: Llewellyn Publications, 2006.

Huson, Paul. *Mystical Origins of the Tarot: From Ancient Roots to Modern Usage*. Rochester, VT: Destiny Books, 2004.

Katz, Marcus. *Tarosophy: Tarot to Engage Life, Not Escape It*. Keswick, UK: Forge Press, 2016.

Matlin, Jenna. *Have Tarot Will Travel: A Comprehensive Guide to Reading at Festivals as a Tarot Professional*. Self-published, 2016.

Nichols, Sallie. *Jung and Tarot: An Archetypal Journey*. San Francisco: Red Wheel/Weiser, 2004.

Pollack, Rachel. *Tarot Wisdom: Spiritual Teachings and Deeper Meanings*. St. Paul, MN: Llewellyn Publications, 2003.

Reed, Theresa, and Shaheen Miro. *Tarot for Troubled Times: Confront Your Shadow, Heal Your Self, Transform the World.* Newburyport, MA: Weiser Books, 2019.

Rosengarten, Arthur. *Tarot and Psychology: Spectrums of Possibility.* St. Paul, MN: Paragon House, 2000.

Thies, Gina G. *Tarot Coupling: Resources & Resolutions for Relationship Readings.* Atglen, PA: Schiffer Publishing, 2013.

Wen, Benebell. *Holistic Tarot: An Integrative Approach to Using Tarot for Personal Growth.* Berkeley, CA: North Atlantic Books, 2015.

Psychology, Science, and Intuition

These books are great foundational material for you both as a practitioner and to explore psychological aspects often encountered in readings.

Buonomano, Dean. *Your Brain Is a Time Machine: The Neuroscience and Physics of Time.* New York: W.W. Norton & Company, 2017.

Burns, David D. *When Panic Attacks: The New Drug-Free Anxiety Therapy That Can Change Your Life.* New York: Random House, 2006.

Campbell, Joseph. *The Hero With a Thousand Faces.* Princeton, NJ: Princeton University Press, 1973.

———. *The Power of Myth.* New York: Anchor Books, 1991.

Chödrön, Pema. *When Things Fall Apart: Heart Advice for Difficult Times.* Boulder, CO: Shambhala Press, 2000.

Cox, Brian, and Jeff Forshaw. *Why Does E = mc²? (And Why Should We Care?).* Boston: First Da Capo Press, 2009.

Day, Laura. *Practical Intuition: How to Harness the Power of Your Instinct and Make It Work for You.* New York: Random House, 1996.

"Flexbar." Theraband website, https://www.theraband.com/theraband-flexbar-resistance-bar.html.

Frankl, Viktor E. *Man's Search for Meaning.* Boston: Beacon Press, 2006.

Jung, Carl. *Synchronicity: An Acausal Connecting Principle.* Princeton, NJ: Princeton University Press, 1969.

Keen, Sam, and Anne Valley-Fox. *Your Mythic Journey: Finding Meaning in Your Life Through Writing and Storytelling*. Los Angeles: Jeremy P. Tarcher, 1989.

Kottler, Jeffrey. *On Being a Therapist*. San Francisco: Jossey-Bass, 2003.

Kushner, Harold. *When Bad Things Happen to Good People*. New York: Anchor Books, 1981.

North, Ora. *I Don't Want to Be an Empath Anymore: How to Reclaim Your Power Over Emotional Overload, Maintain Boundaries, and Live Your Best Life*. Oakland, CA: Reveal Press, 2019.

Rosenberg, Marshall. *Nonviolent Communication: A Language of Life*. Encinitas, CA: Puddledancer Press, 2003.

Schwartz, Arielle. *The Complex PTSD Workbook: A Mind-Body Approach to Regaining Emotional Control & Becoming Whole*. Berkeley, CA: Althea Press, 2016.

Sorensen, Michael S. *I Hear You: The Surprisingly Simple Skill Behind Extraordinary Relationships*. Alpine, UT: Autumn Creek Press, 2017.

Van Der Kolk, Bessel. *The Body Keeps the Score: Brain, Mind, and Body in the Healing of Trauma*. New York: Penguin Books, 2014.

Wallin, David. *Attachment in Psychotherapy*. New York: Guilford Press, 2007.

Energy and Magick

These are great resources for specifically the clearing and protection of your energy.

Matthews, Caitlin. *Psychic Shield: The Personal Handbook of Psychic Protection*. Berkeley, CA: Ulysses Press, 2006.

Hall, Judy. *The Encyclopedia of Crystals*. London: Octopus Publishing Group, 2013.

Linn, Denise. *Sacred Space: Clearing and Enhancing the Energy of Your Home*. London: Random House, 1995.

Welch, Michelle. *The Magic of Connection: Stop Cutting Cords & Learn to Transform Negative Energy to Live an Empowered Life*. Woodbury, MN: Llewellyn Publications, 2021.

Bibliography

Alexander, Courtney. *Dust II Onyx*. Self-Published, 2016.

Bakens, Martien. *The Fifth Tarot*. Nevada City, NV: Blue Dolphin Publishing, 2008.

Burgoon, Judee K., Lesa A. Stern, and Leesa Dillman. *Interpersonal Adaptation: Dyadic Interaction Patterns*. Cambridge, MA: Cambridge University Press, 1995.

Burns, David D. *Feeling Good: The New Mood Therapy*. New York: Avon Books, 1980.

Campbell, Joseph. *Myths to Live By: How We Recreate Ancient Legends in our Daily Lives to Release Human Potential*. New York: Bantam Books, 1972.

Cunningham, Scott. *Magical Herbalism: The Secret Craft of the Wise*. St. Paul, MN: Llewellyn Publications, 1982.

Cohen, Raymond. *Negotiating Across Cultures: International Communication in an Interdependent World* (rev. ed.). Washington, DC: United States Institute of Peace, 2004.

Cox, Brian, and Jeffrey Forshaw. *Why Does E = mc^2? (And Why Should We Care?)*. Cambridge, MA: Da Capo Press, 2009.

Craig, William Lane. "Divine Foreknowledge and Newcomb's Paradox." *Philosophia* 17, no. 3 (1987): 331–350.

Cynova, Melissa. *Kitchen Table Tarot: Pull Up a Chair, Shuffle the Cards, and Let's Talk Tarot*. Woodbury, MN: Llewellyn Publications, 2017.

Dawn, Ethony. *Your Tarot Court: Read Any Deck with Confidence*. Woodbury, MN: Llewellyn Publications, 2019.

"DEVIL CARD CONFESSION; THE KILLER CAUGHT BY A TAROT READER; I turned over the Blasted Tower, the Emperor & then the Devil.. & he said 'It's terrible, I killed him'; EXCLUSIVE." Retrieved July 5, 2021 from the Free Library website. https://www .thefreelibrary.com/DEVIL+CARD+CONFESSION%3b+THE +KILLER+CAUGHT+BY+A+TAROT+READER%3b+I+turned ...-a0453503943.

Dominguez, Ivo Jr. *Spirit Speak: Knowing and Understanding Spirit Guides, Ancestors, Ghosts, Angels, and the Divine.* Franklin Lakes, NJ: New Page Books, 2008.

"Word Cloud Generator." Fun Generators website, https://fungenerators .com/word-cloud/.

Gray, Eden. *The Complete Guide to the Tarot: Determine Your Destiny! Predict Your Own Future!* New York: Crown Publishers, 1970.

Greer, Mary, and Tom Little. *Understanding the Tarot Court.* St. Paul, MN: Llewellyn Publications, 2004.

Hawn, Harley. "Time Sense: Polychronicity and Monochronicity," originally published March 27, 2005. http://www.harley.com/writing/time-sense .php.

Gentile, John S. "Epilogue: The Mythic Storyteller: Word-Power and Ambivalence." *Storytelling, Self, Society* 7, no. 2 (2011): 148–160. http:// www.jstor.org/stable/41949156.

Lindquist, Jay D., and Carol Kaufman-Scarborough. "The Polychronic— Monochronic Tendency Model: PMTS Scale Development and Vali- dation." *Time & Society* 16, no. 2–3 (September 2007): 253–285. https:// doi.org/10.1177/0961463X07080270.

Lobo, Francisco, Paulo Crawford. "Time, Closed Timelike Curves and Causality." *The Nature of Time: Geometry, Physics and Perception.* NATO Science Series II, 95 (2003): 289–296.

"Questioning Techniques: Asking Questions Effectively." Mind Tools website, https://www.mindtools.com/pages/article/newTMC_88.htm, 2018.

Oettingen, Gabriele. *Rethinking Positive Thinking: Inside the New Science of Motivation*. New York: Random House, 2014.

Sinha, Chris, Vera da Silva Sinha, Jörg Zinken, and Wany Sampaio. "When Time Is Not Space: The Social and Linguistic Construction of Time Intervals and Temporal Event Relations in an Amazonian Culture." *Language and Cognition* 3, no. 1 (2011): 137–169. doi:10.1515 /langcog.2011.006.

Sterle, Lisa. *Modern Witch Tarot*. New York: Sterling Ethos, 2019.

Waite, Arthur. *The Pictorial Key to the Tarot*. York Beach, ME: Weiser, 1983. First published 1911 by William Rider & Son (London).

Warwick-Smith, Kate. *The Tarot Court Cards: Archetypal Patterns of Relationship in the Minor Arcana*. Rochester, NY: Destiny Books, 2003.

To Write to the Author

If you wish to contact the author or would like more information about this book, please write to the author in care of Llewellyn Worldwide Ltd. and we will forward your request. Both the author and publisher appreciate hearing from you and learning of your enjoyment of this book and how it has helped you. Llewellyn Worldwide Ltd. cannot guarantee that every letter written to the author can be answered, but all will be forwarded. Please write to:

Jenna Matlin
℅ Llewellyn Worldwide
2143 Wooddale Drive
Woodbury, MN 55125-2989

Please enclose a self-addressed stamped envelope for reply,
or $1.00 to cover costs. If outside the U.S.A., enclose
an international postal reply coupon.

Many of Llewellyn's authors have websites with additional information and resources. For more information, please visit our website at http://www.llewellyn.com.